200 deliciou s

hamlyn | all colour cookbook

200 delicious desserts

Sara Lewis

For Sian, a few ideas to help broaden your repertoire!

An Hachette UK Company
www.hachette.co.uk

First published in Great Britain in 2009 by
Hamlyn, a division of Octopus Publishing Group Ltd,
2–4 Heron Quays, London E14 4JP
www.octopusbooks.co.uk

Copyright © Octopus Publishing Group Ltd 2009

Some of the recipes in this book have previously appeared
in other books published by Hamlyn.

ISBN: 978-0-600-61930-7

A CIP catalogue record for this book is available
from the British Library.

Printed and bound in China

1 2 3 4 5 6 7 8 9 10

Both metric and imperial measurements are given in all
recipes. Use one set of measurements, not a mixture of both.

Standard level spoon measurements are used in all recipes
1 tablespoon = one 15 ml spoon
1 teaspoon = one 5 ml spoon

Ovens should be preheated to the specified temperature – if
using a fan-assisted oven, follow the manufacturer's
instructions for adjusting the time and the temperature.

Milk should be full fat unless otherwise stated.

Eggs should be medium unless otherwise stated. The
Department of Health advises that eggs should not be
consumed raw. This book contains some dishes made with
raw or lightly cooked eggs. It is prudent for vulnerable
people such as pregnant and nursing mothers, invalids, the
elderly, babies and young children to avoid uncooked or
lightly cooked dishes made with eggs. Once prepared, these
dishes should be kept refrigerated and used promptly.

This book also includes dishes made with nuts and nut
derivatives. It is advisable for those with known allergic
reactions to nuts and nut derivatives and those who may be
potentially vulnerable to these allergies, such as pregnant
and nursing mothers, invalids, the elderly, babies and
children to avoid dishes made with nuts and nut oils. It is
also prudent to check the labels of pre–prepared ingredients
for the possible inclusion of nut derivatives.

contents

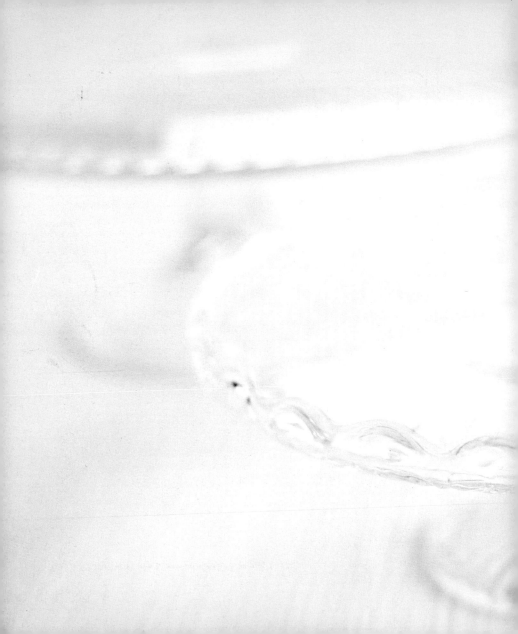

introduction

introduction

Not many people can resist a dessert. A good one will cheer you up after a bad day at work, banish the blues and make a grand finale to a special meal or a welcome alternative gift to a bunch of flowers when visiting friends for supper. And with over 200 recipes in this book, there's something here for everyone.

Those who need a chocolate fix can choose from such decadent delights as Double Chocolate Puddings (see page 38), hot from the oven and drizzled with white chocolate cream, or a slice of rich gooey Chocolate & Marshmallow Torte (see page 42). If you're a pastry fan, try the melt in-the-mouth Freeform Apple & Mixed Berry Pie (see page 70) or the Deep Dish Puff Apple Pie (see page 90). Alternatively, if you are watching your weight, there are even healthy

fresh-fruit recipes, such the Green Fruit Salad (see page 204).

Short of time? You can cheat and use shop-bought puff or sweet shortcrust pastry to make impressive desserts like Peach & Blueberry Jalousie (see page 64), Cherry Frangipane Tart (see page 82) or the comforting Lemon Meringue Pie (see page 74). Even easier is a biscuit crumb case, such as Banoffee Pie (see page 108). There's a whole chapter called 'Last-minute Quickies', full of ideas for desserts that can be whipped up in no more than 10–20 minutes, such as Tamarind & Mango Sundae (see page 200) or Mini Baked Alaskas (see page 218).

If you like to get organized in advance, try one of the frozen recipes in the 'Chilled Out' chapter, such as Lime & Passion Fruit Crunch Tart (see page 164) or Mint Granita (see page 180). These ice-cold treats are perfect after a barbecue in the garden or a hot curry in the winter.

These days, our busy schedules mean a homemade pudding is a treat rather than an everyday occurrence, but when you do have the time to make one it is not only immensely rewarding but also a great way to unwind.

Pages 9–14 describe the dessert-making techniques: whisking eggs and sugar, folding in, working with chocolate, making meringues, lining a pastry case and decorating a pie. On page 15 you'll find recipes for homemade flaky and sweet shortcrust pastry.

whisking eggs and sugar

When making mousses, chilled soufflés, sabayon sauce, zabaglione, a Swiss roll or a sponge flan case, the recipe will call for the eggs and sugar to be whisked until the whisk leaves a trail when lifted above the mixture. This is best done with a hand-held electric mixer held over a bowl of eggs and sugar set over a saucepan of gently simmering water. The hot water helps to speed up the whisking process and increase the volume of air trapped in the eggs and sugar. (If you have a fixed mixer, do this on the work surface; it will just take a little longer.)

Three eggs will take 8–10 minutes to whisk until thick. To test when the mixture is ready, lift the whisk out of the mixture and try to drizzle a zigzag as the mixture falls from the whisk – if this stays on the surface for a few seconds, the mixture is ready.

whisking cream

Many people tend to overwhip double or whipping cream. The secret is to whisk the double cream until it just begins to form soft swirls, as it will thicken slightly as it stands. Overwhipping makes the cream take on a grainy, almost buttery texture and spoils the finish of the pudding.

folding in

Once a whisked mixture is ready, you will need to fold in puréed fruit, whipped cream or melted chocolate for a chilled soufflé or mousse or sifted flour for a whisked sponge.

Use a large-bowled spoon (a serving spoon is ideal) and gently cut and turn the spoon through the mixture in a figure-of-eight movement. Try to be as gentle as you can so that you don't knock out all the air you have just worked so hard to incorporate.

making meringues

The bowl and whisk must both be dry and completely grease-free. If you drop any yolk at all into the whites when separating the eggs, scoop it out with a piece of shell, as even the tiniest amount of yolk will prevent the whites from whisking.

1 Whisk the whites until very thick so they will stand in moist-looking peaks. If you're not sure whether they're ready, turn the bowl upside down – if the egg whites stay put, they're ready; if they begin to slide or fall out, whisk a little more.

2 Gradually whisk in the sugar a teaspoonful at a time. It may sound a slow process, but it makes for very thick meringue. When all the sugar has been added, whisk for a couple of minutes more until the meringue is very thick and glossy.

3 Shape the meringues by spooning or spreading on to a baking sheet lined with nonstick baking paper, and bake according to the recipe until the meringues are crisp and may be easily lifted off the paper. If they stick to the paper, they aren't ready. Return to the oven for 10–20 minutes and test again.

working with chocolate

To melt chocolate, break it into pieces and heat for 5 minutes or so in a bowl set over a saucepan of very gently simmering water, making sure that the water doesn't touch the base of the bowl. Stir just before using.

Decorative chocolate curls are easy to make using a swivel-bladed vegetable peeler. Place a bar of chocolate on a chopping board with the smooth underside uppermost. Run the vegetable peeler blade along the top of the chocolate with the handle almost touching the edge of the bar. If the curls are very small, warm the chocolate in 10-second bursts in the microwave on full power (or in a warm oven) and try again. As the chocolate softens, the curls will increase in size.

lining a pastry case

A loose-based flan tin makes it easy to remove the finished tart after baking.

1 Roll out the pastry on a lightly floured surface until a little larger than the tin.

2 Lift the pastry over a rolling pin and drape into the tin. Press over the base and up the sides of the tin with your fingertips, taking care where the sides meet the base of the tin.

3 Trim off the excess pastry with a rolling pin or small knife, then press the pastry slightly above the top of the tin. Chill for 15 minutes or longer if you have time, to minimize shrinkage before cooking.

baking blind

This rather strange term really just means to bake the tart case empty.

1 Stand the tart tin on a baking sheet, then prick the pastry base with a fork.

2 Line with crumpled nonstick or greaseproof paper. Half-fill the tin with dried macaroni or baking beans to hold the pastry in shape.

3 Bake at 190°C (375°F), Gas Mark 5, for 10–15 minutes until just set, then lift out the paper and filling. Cook the empty tart for 5 more minutes until golden around the top edges and the base is dry and crisp, or for 10 minutes if the filling will not be cooked.

covering and decorating a pie

For a professional finish to a puff, flaky or shortcrust topped fruit pie.

1 Cut a narrow strip of pastry from the edges of the rolled-out dough the same width as the rim of the pie dish. Brush the dish rim with water, beaten egg or milk and stick the strips in place, butting ends of strips together until the rim is completely covered.

2 Lift the remaining pastry over a rolling pin and drape over the top of the pie. Press the edges together then trim off the excess pastry with a small knife.

3 Knock up the edges of the pie by making small horizontal cuts around the pastry rim. This helps to encourage the puff pastry layers to separate and rise during baking and can also give the impression of layers in a shortcrust pie.

4 Flute the edges by pressing the first and second finger on to the pie edge, then make small cuts with a knife between them to create a scalloped edge. Repeat all the way around the pie.

5 Brush the pie with a little beaten egg or milk to glaze it. To decorate with pastry leaves, roll out trimmings, cut a strip about 2.5 cm (1 inch) wide, then cut out diamond shapes. Mark veins with a knife and curl the ends of the leaf. Press on to the glazed pie, then brush over a little more glazing.

6 Alternatively, hearts, circles, festive shapes or numbers can be stamped from rerolled pastry trimmings with small biscuit cutters, then arranged on the glazed pie and glazed with a little more beaten egg or milk.

sweet shortcrust pastry

A great all-round pastry, versatile and quick to make, it is ideal for tart cases, freeform pies or double-crust pies. This recipe makes enough to fill a 25 cm (10 inch) flan tin or 450 g (14½ oz) pastry.

250 g (8 oz) **plain flour**, plus extra for dusting
25 g (1 oz) **icing sugar**
125 g (4 oz) mix of **unsalted butter** and
white vegetable fat, or all butter, diced
8–9 teaspoons cold **water**

Place the flour and sugar in a bowl, add the sugar and diced fats and rub the fats into the flour by lifting up small amounts with the fingers and thumbs and pressing the thumbs over the fingertips to break the fats into tiny pieces. Continue until the mixture resembles fine breadcrumbs. (For speed, use an electric mixer or food processor.) Add 8 teaspoons cold water and mix with a round-bladed knife until the crumbs begin to clump together, then squeeze with the fingertips, adding an extra teaspoon of water if needed to bring the mixture together to a ball. Knead lightly on a lightly floured surface then chill, wrapped in clingfilm, for 15 minutes, or if preferred roll out, line a tart tin and chill. If chilled, the pastry relaxes and shrinks less when baked.

flaky pastry

Supermarket puff pastry is so good, and homemade puff pastry so hard to get right, that it is not really worth making it yourself. Flaky pastry is much quicker and easier to make and this light crumbly pastry is perfect to top a deep-dish pie (such as Deep Dish Puff Apple Pie, see page 90) or to use for a jalousie-style double-crust pie or for individual pastries. This recipe makes enough to top a 1.2 litre (2 pint) pie dish or 500 g (1 lb) pastry.

250 g (8 oz) **plain flour**, plus extra for dusting
pinch **salt**
75 g (3 oz) **lard** or **white pastry fat**
75 g (3 oz) **unsalted butter**
2 teaspoons **lemon juice**
5–6 tablespoons cold **water**

Place the flour and salt in a mixing bowl, add one quarter of the white fat and one quarter of the butter and rub in with the fingertips until the mixture resembles fine breadcrumbs. Add the lemon juice then enough cold water, mixing with a round-bladed knife, to form a soft but not sticky dough. Knead lightly, then roll out on a floured surface to form a rough rectangle, about 46 x 15 cm (18 x 6 inches). Dot half the remaining white fat and butter over the bottom two-thirds of the pastry. Fold over the top one-third of the dough and then fold up the bottom third to enclose the fat. Press the edges together well, then give the dough a quarter turn. Roll out the pastry again, dot with fats and fold, as before. Give a quarter turn, then roll and fold twice more. Wrap in clingfilm and chill for 30 minutes.

winter warmers

lemon puddle pudding

Serves **4**
Preparation time **20 minutes**
Cooking time **25 minutes**

75 g (3 oz) **unsalted butter**,
   at room temperature
150 g (5 oz) **caster sugar**
grated rind of 2 **lemons**, plus
   juice from 1 lemon
3 **eggs**, separated
50 g (2 oz) **self-raising flour**
300 ml (½ pint) **milk**
icing sugar, for dusting
   (optional)

Grease a 1.2 litre (2 pint) pie dish lightly, then stand the dish in a roasting tin. Put the rest of the butter in a mixing bowl with the sugar and lemon rind. Whisk the egg whites in a separate bowl until they are softly peaking. Using the still dirty whisk, beat the butter, sugar and lemon rind until light and fluffy, then mix in the flour and egg yolks.

Mix in the milk and lemon juice gradually until only just mixed. The mixture may appear to separate slightly but this will disappear during baking.

Fold in the egg whites, then gently pour the mix into the greased dish. Pour hot water from the tap into the roasting tin to come halfway up the sides of the dish.

Cook in a preheated oven, 190°C (375°F), Gas Mark 5, for about 25 minutes until slightly risen, golden brown and the top has begun to crack. Insert a knife into the centre – the top two-thirds should be soufflé-like and the bottom third a saucy, custard-like layer. If it's very soft in the centre, cook for an extra 5 minutes.

Dust the top with a little sifted icing sugar, if liked, then serve immediately spooned into shallow bowls. Don't leave the dessert to stand or the topping will absorb the sauce.

For Grand Marnier pudding, use the grated rind of 1 large orange instead of the lemon rind and replace the lemon juice with 3 tablespoons Grand Marnier. Cook as above.

roasted pears with oriental spices

Serves **4**
Preparation time **20 minutes**
Cooking time **25 minutes**

4 **pears**
8 tablespoons **dry** or **sweet**
   sherry
8 tablespoons **water**
6–8 pieces **star anise**
1 **cinnamon stick**, broken
   into pieces
8 **cloves**
8 **cardamom pods**, crushed
50 g (2 oz) **unsalted butter**
4 tablespoons **light**
   muscovado sugar
1 **orange**

Leave the peel on the pears and cut them in half, down through the stems to the base. Scoop out the core, then put in a roasting tin with the cut sides up. Spoon the sherry into the core cavity of each pear and the water into the base of the tin. Sprinkle the spices over the pears, including the cardamom pods and their black seeds. Dot with the butter, then sprinkle with the sugar.

Remove the rind from the orange and sprinkle into the tin. Cut the orange into wedges and squeeze the juice over the pears. Add the wedges to the base of the roasting tin.

Cook in a preheated oven, 180°C (350°F), Gas Mark 4, for 25 minutes until tender and just beginning to brown, spooning the pan juices over the pears halfway through cooking and again at the end.

Spoon into shallow dishes, drizzle with the pan juices and serve with crème fraîche or Greek yogurt.

For roast apples with peppercorns, core and halve 4 dessert apples, then place, cut side up, in a roasting tin. Spoon 200 ml (7 fl oz) cider over the apples and into the roasting tin. Sprinkle with 1 teaspoon coarsely crushed multicoloured peppercorns and 1 broken cinnamon stick. Dot with butter and sprinkle with sugar as above. Remove the rind from 1 lemon and reserve for decoration, then cut the lemon into wedges, squeeze the juice over the apples and add the wedges to the base of the tin. Bake as above.

sticky toffee puddings

Makes **8**
Preparation time **20 minutes**
Cooking time **45–50 minutes**

125 g (4 oz) pitted chopped
  dried dates
150 ml (¼ pint) **water**
125 g (4 oz) **unsalted butter**,
  softened
125 g (4 oz) **caster sugar**
1 teaspoon **vanilla essence**
3 **eggs**
175 g (6 oz) **self-raising flour**
1 teaspoon **baking powder**

Toffee sauce
300 ml (½ pint) **double cream**
125 g (4 oz) **light brown
  sugar**
50 g (2 oz) **unsalted butter**

Put the dates in a small pan with the measured water and simmer gently for 5 minutes until the dates are soft and pulpy. Blend to a purée, then allow to cool.

Make the sauce. Heat half the cream in a small, heavy-bottomed pan with the sugar and butter until the sugar dissolves. Bring to the boil, then let the sauce bubble for about 5 minutes until a rich, dark caramel. Stir in the remaining cream and set aside.

Grease 8 metal 200 ml (7 fl oz) pudding moulds and line the bottoms with nonstick baking paper. Beat the butter, sugar, vanilla essence, eggs, flour and baking powder in a bowl for 1–2 minutes until pale and creamy. Stir the date purée into the pudding mixture.

Divide the mixture among the moulds. Level the tops and place in a roasting tin. Pour boiling water to a depth of 1.5 cm (¾ inch) in the tin and cover with foil. Bake in a preheated oven, 180°C (350°F), Gas Mark 4, for 35–40 minutes or until risen and firm to the touch.

Leave the puddings in the moulds while you reheat the sauce, then loosen the edges of the moulds and invert the puddings on to serving plates. Cover with sauce and serve with additional cream or ice cream.

For gingered figgy puddings, cook 125 g (4 oz) diced dried figs in the water in place of the dates. Make the sauce and puddings as above, adding 2 tablespoons chopped glacé ginger to the beaten pudding mix.

choco bread & butter pudding

Serves **4**

Preparation time **20 minutes**, plus standing

Cooking time **25 minutes**

4 **chocolate croissants**
50 g (2 oz) **unsalted butter**
50 g (2 oz) **caster sugar**
¼ teaspoon **ground mixed spice**
300 ml (½ pint) **milk**
4 **eggs**
1 teaspoon **vanilla essence**
icing sugar, to decorate

Grease a 1.2 litre (2 pint) shallow, round, ovenproof pie dish. Slice the croissants thickly and spread the butter over one side of each cut face of croissant. Stand the croissant slices upright and close together in the dish to completely fill it.

Mix the sugar and spice together, then spoon over the croissants and between the gaps. Stand the dish in a large roasting tin.

Beat the milk, eggs and vanilla essence together, then strain into the dish. Leave to stand for 15 minutes.

Pour hot water from the tap into the roasting tin to come halfway up the sides of the pie dish. Bake in a preheated oven, 180°C (350°F), Gas Mark 4, for about 25 minutes until the pudding is golden and the custard just set.

Lift the dish out of the roasting tin, dust with sifted icing sugar and serve the pudding warm with a little pouring cream.

For fruited bread & butter pudding, lightly butter 8 slices of white bread, cut into triangles and arrange in slightly overlapping layers in the dish, sprinkling with 75 g (3 oz) luxury dried fruit between the layers. Add the sugar as above, but omit the mixed spice. Mix the eggs, milk and vanilla, pour over the bread, then continue as above.

hot blackberry & apple trifle

Serves **4**
Preparation time **20 minutes**,
  plus cooling
Cooking time **20–25 minutes**

150 g (5 oz) **fresh** or **frozen**
  blackberries
2 **dessert apples**, cored,
  unpeeled and sliced
1 tablespoon **water**
50 g (2 oz) **caster sugar**
4 **trifle sponges**
3 tablespoons **dry** or **sweet**
  sherry
425 g (14 oz) can or carton
  custard

Meringue
3 **egg whites**
75 g (3 oz) **caster sugar**

Put the blackberries, apples, measured water and sugar in a saucepan, then cover and simmer for 5 minutes or until the fruit has softened. Leave the mixture to cool slightly.

Break the trifle sponges into chunks and arrange in an even layer in the base of a 1.2 litre (2 pint) ovenproof pie or soufflé dish and drizzle with the sherry. Spoon the poached fruit and syrup over the top, then cover with custard.

Whisk the egg whites in a large, dry bowl until stiffly peaking, then gradually whisk in the sugar, a teaspoonful at a time, until the meringue is stiff and glossy (see page 10). Spoon over the custard and swirl the top with the back of a spoon.

Bake in a preheated oven, 180°C (350°F), Gas Mark 4, for 15–20 minutes until heated through and the meringue is golden. Serve immediately.

For apple mallow, peel, core and thickly slice 8 dessert apples, then simmer in a saucepan with the grated rind and juice of 1 lemon, 4 cloves and 25 g (1 oz) caster sugar until tender. Spoon into a 1.2 litre (2 pint) ovenproof dish. Make the meringue as above, adding ¼ teaspoon ground cinnamon with the sugar. Spoon over the fruit, then bake as above. Serve the mallow warm.

vanilla soufflés & apricot coulis

Serves **8**
Preparation time **25 minutes**
Cooking time **25 minutes**

75 g (3 oz) **caster sugar**, plus
   extra for dusting
200 g (7 oz) **ready-to-eat
   dried apricots**, coarsely
   chopped
125 ml (4 fl oz) **water**, plus
   1 tablespoon
3 tablespoons **cornflour**
5 tablespoons **Cointreau** or
   other **orange-flavoured
   liqueur**
150 ml (¼ pint) **milk**
1 teaspoon **vanilla essence**
125 ml (4 fl oz) **double cream**
4 **eggs**, separated
icing sugar, for dusting

Grease 8 ramekin dishes and dust each one lightly with caster sugar. Put the apricots in a small pan with the measured water and simmer gently for 3 minutes until softened. Blend ½ teaspoon of the cornflour with 1 tablespoon water and add it to the pan. Cook gently for 1 minute or until the sauce has thickened.

Put the mixture in a food processor or blender, add the liqueur and blend until smooth. Divide the mixture among the ramekins.

Blend the remaining cornflour in a pan with a little of the milk. Add the remaining milk and heat gently, stirring, until thickened. Stir in 50 g (2 oz) of the caster sugar, the vanilla essence, cream and egg yolks and put in a large bowl.

Beat the egg whites until peaking and gradually beat in the remaining caster sugar. Using a large metal spoon, fold the egg whites into the custard.

Spoon the mixture into the ramekins and put them on a baking sheet. Bake in a preheated oven, 200°C (400°F), Gas Mark 6, for 20 minutes or until well risen. Dust with sifted icing sugar and serve immediately.

For apple & Calvados soufflés, peel, core and dice 4 dessert apples. Place in a small saucepan with 2 tablespoons water, cover and cook for 10 minutes until soft. Divide between 8 greased and sugared ramekins. Make the soufflés as above, adding 5 tablespoons Calvados or ordinary brandy instead of the Cointreau.

jam roly-poly

Serves **6**
Preparation time **25 minutes**
Cooking time **2 hours**

300 g (10 oz) **self-raising flour**
1 teaspoon **baking powder**
150 g (5 oz) **shredded vegetable suet**
75 g (3 oz) **caster sugar**
50 g (2 oz) **fresh breadcrumbs**
finely grated rind of 1 **lemon**
finely grated rind of 1 **orange**
1 **egg**, beaten
175–200 ml (6–7 fl oz) **milk**
6 tablespoons **raspberry jam**
150 g (5 oz) **frozen raspberries**, just defrosted

Put the flour, baking powder, suet and sugar in a bowl, then stir in the breadcrumbs and fruit rinds. Add the egg, then gradually mix in enough milk to make a soft but not sticky dough.

Knead lightly, then roll out to a 30 cm (12 inch) square. Spread with the jam, leaving a 2.5 cm (1 inch) border, then sprinkle the raspberries on top. Brush the border with a little milk, then roll up the pastry. Wrap loosely in a large piece of nonstick baking paper, twisting the edges together and leaving a little space for the pudding to rise, then wrap loosely in foil.

Put on a roasting rack set over a large roasting tin, then pour boiling water into the tin but not over the roasting rack. Cover the tin with foil and twist over the edges to seal well, then bake in a preheated oven, 150°C (300°F), Gas Mark 2, for 2 hours until the pudding is well risen. Check once or twice during baking and top up the water level if needed.

Transfer the pudding to a chopping board using a teacloth. Unwrap, cut into thick slices and serve with hot custard.

For spotted dick, warm 3 tablespoons orange juice or rum in a small saucepan, add 150 g (5 oz) raisins, 1 teaspoon ground ginger and ¼ teaspoon grated nutmeg and leave to soak for 1 hour or longer. Add to the flour mix just before adding the egg and milk. Shape into a long sausage, wrap in paper and foil and steam in the oven as above. Serve sliced with custard flavoured with a little extra rum, if liked.

apricot queen of puddings

Serves **6**
Preparation time **25 minutes**,
  plus standing
Cooking time **35–45 minutes**

600 ml (1 pint) **milk**
grated rind of 2 **lemons**
50 g (2 oz) **unsalted butter**
175 g (6 oz) **caster sugar**
100 g (3½ oz) **fresh**
  breadcrumbs
4 **eggs**, separated
4 tablespoons **apricot jam**
125 g (4 oz) ready-to-eat
  dried apricots, diced

Pour the milk into a saucepan, add the lemon rind and bring just to the boil. Take off the heat and stir in the butter and 50 g (2 oz) of the sugar until the butter has melted and the sugar dissolved. Mix in the breadcrumbs and leave to stand for 15 minutes.

Mix the egg yolks into the milk mixture, then pour into a greased 1.5 litre (2½ pint) ovenproof pie dish. Bake in a preheated oven, 180°C (350°F), Gas Mark 4, for 20–25 minutes until the custard has set and is just beginning to brown around the edges.

Dot the jam over the baked custard and sprinkle with the diced apricots. Whisk the egg whites in a large bowl until stiffly peaking, then gradually whisk in the remaining sugar a teaspoonful at a time until thick and glossy (see page 10). Spoon over the jam, then swirl with the back of the spoon.

Put the dish back in the oven for 15–20 minutes until the meringue is golden and cooked through. Serve warm with cream.

For Monmouth pudding, warm the milk as above, adding ¼ teaspoon grated nutmeg instead of the fruit rinds. Add the butter and breadcrumbs as above with 125 g (4 oz) caster sugar. After the mixture has been left to stand, stir in the egg yolks. Whisk the whites (but do not add any more sugar) and fold into the milk mixture. Spoon 4 tablespoons strawberry or raspberry jam into the base of the pie dish, pour the milk mixture over the top and bake as above for 30–35 minutes until set and golden. Serve with extra jam.

steamed pudding with mango

Serves **6**

Preparation time **20 minutes**, plus standing

Cooking time **1 hour 40 minutes**

1 medium **mango**, cut into chunks

2 tablespoons **ready-made** or **homemade vanilla syrup** (see below), plus extra for serving

125 g (4 oz) **unsalted butter**, softened

125 g (4 oz) **caster sugar**

1 teaspoon **vanilla essence**

2 **eggs**

175 g (6 oz) **self-raising flour**

4 tablespoons **unsweetened dessicated coconut**

1 tablespoon **milk**

Grease a 1.2 litre (2 pint) pudding basin and line the bottom with a circle of nonstick baking paper. Scatter the mango chunks in the prepared bowl and drizzle with the vanilla syrup.

Put the butter, sugar, vanilla essence, eggs and flour in a bowl and beat for 1–2 minutes until creamy. Stir in the coconut and milk, then spoon the mixture into the pudding basin. Level the surface.

Cover the bowl with a double thickness of pleated nonstick baking paper and secure under the rim with string. Cover with foil, tucking the edges firmly under the rim.

Put the bowl in a steamer or large pan. Half-fill the pan with boiling water and cover with a tight-fitting lid. Steam gently for 1 hour 40 minutes, topping up the water as necessary, then allow to stand for 10 minutes.

Invert the pudding on to a serving plate and drizzle with extra vanilla syrup.

For vanilla syrup, put 150 g (5 oz) caster sugar in a small heavy-bottomed pan with 125 ml (4 fl oz) water, and heat gently until the sugar dissolves. Boil for 6–8 minutes until the syrup is golden. Immediately dip the bottom of the pan into cold water to stop cooking. Add 125 ml (4 fl oz) hot water and 2 vanilla pods slit along their length (and, if liked, a cinnamon stick or a few whole cloves). Reheat to mix in the extra water. Leave until cooled, then pour into a clean bottle. Seal and shake the bottle to bring out the vanilla flavour. Store for several days and shake before use.

steamed apple pudding

Serves **4**
Preparation time **20 minutes**
Cooking time **2 hours**

125 g (4 oz) **unsalted butter**
4 tablespoons **golden syrup**
2 **cooking apples**, about
500 g (1 lb) in total, cored
and peeled
100 g (3½ oz) **caster sugar**
2 **eggs**, beaten
200 g (7 oz) **self-raising flour**
grated rind of 1 **orange**, and
3 tablespoons of the juice

Grease the inside of a 1.2 litre (2 pint) pudding basin lightly and line the base with a small circle of nonstick baking paper. Spoon in the syrup, then thickly slice 1 apple and arrange in an even layer on top. Coarsely grate the remaining apple.

Cream the butter and sugar in a bowl until pale and creamy. Gradually mix in alternate spoonfuls of beaten egg and flour until both have all been added and the mixture is smooth.

Stir in the grated apple, orange rind and juice, then spoon into the pudding basin. Level the surface and cover with a piece of pleated nonstick baking paper and foil. Tie in place with string, adding a string handle.

Lower the basin into the top of a steamer set over a saucepan of simmering water, cover with a lid and steam for 2 hours until the pudding is well risen and a knife comes out cleanly when inserted into the centre of the sponge.

Remove the foil and paper, loosen the edge of the pudding and turn out on to a plate with a rim. Serve immediately with custard or ice cream.

For cranberry & orange steamed pudding, cook 150 g (5 oz) frozen cranberries in a saucepan with the juice of 1 orange for 5 minutes until softened. Spoon 2 tablespoons raspberry jam into the prepared pudding basin, then add the cranberries. Make the sponge as above with 1 peeled, cored and grated cooking apple, also adding the grated rind of 1 orange. Cover and steam as above.

double chocolate puddings

Serves **6**
Preparation time **25 minutes**
Cooking time **18–20 minutes**

125 g (4 oz) **unsalted butter**,
at room temperature, or
soft margarine
125 g (4 oz) **light muscovado**
sugar
100 g (3½ oz) **self-raising**
flour
15 g (½ oz) **cocoa powder**
2 **eggs**
75 g (3 oz) or 12 squares
plain dark chocolate
100 g (3½ oz) **white**
chocolate, broken into
pieces
150 ml (¼ pint) **double cream**
¼ teaspoon **vanilla essence**

Put the butter or margarine, sugar, flour, cocoa and eggs into a mixing bowl or food processor and beat together until smooth. Divide the mixture between 6 greased sections of a deep muffin tin, then press 2 squares of dark chocolate into each and cover with the pudding mixture.

Bake in a preheated oven, 180°C (350°F), Gas Mark 4, for 18–20 minutes until well risen, slightly crusty around the edges and the centre springs back when pressed with a fingertip.

Meanwhile, warm the white chocolate, cream and vanilla essence together in a small saucepan, stirring until the chocolate has completely melted.

Loosen the edges of the baked puddings with a round-bladed knife, then turn out and transfer to shallow serving bowls. Drizzle with the white chocolate cream and serve immediately.

For walnut & chocolate puddings, omit the cocoa powder from the puddings and mix the butter, sugar and eggs with 125 g (4 oz) self-raising flour, 50 g (2 oz) roughly chopped walnuts and 2 level teaspoons instant coffee dissolved in 3 teaspoons boiling water. Spoon into the muffin tin and press the chocolate squares into the centre of each one as above. Bake as above and serve with pouring cream.

rice pudding with drunken raisins

Serves **4**

Preparation time **10 minutes**, plus soaking

Cooking time **2 hours**

50 g (2 oz) **raisins**

2 tablespoons **fortified wine** (such as **Pedro Ximénez, Madeira** or **sweet sherry**)

25 g (1 oz) **unsalted butter**, diced

65 g (2½ oz) **pudding rice**

25 g (1 oz) **caster sugar**

600 ml (1 pint) **milk**

large pinch of grated **nutmeg** and **cinnamon**

Put the raisins in a small saucepan with the fortified wine and warm together, or microwave the raisins and wine in a small bowl for 30 seconds on full power. Leave to soak for 30 minutes or longer if time allows.

Grease a 900 ml (1½ pint) pie dish, then put in the rice and the sugar. Spoon the soaked raisins on top, then cover with the milk. Dot with the butter and sprinkle with the spices.

Cook in a preheated oven, 150°C (300°F), Gas Mark 2, for 2 hours until the pudding is golden on top, the rice is tender and the milk thick and creamy. Spoon into bowls and serve with spoonfuls of extra-thick cream.

For traditional rice pudding, omit the raisins and fortified wine and add the rice and sugar to the greased pie dish. Pour over 450 ml (¾ pint) milk and 150 ml (¼ pint) double cream. Dot with butter as above, then sprinkle with just-grated nutmeg. Bake, then serve with spoonfuls of strawberry jam.

chocolate & marshmallow torte

Serves **8**
Preparation time **40 minutes**,
   plus cooling
Cooking time **25–30 minutes**

200 g (7 oz) **plain dark
   chocolate**, broken into
   pieces
100 g (3½ oz) **unsalted butter**
5 **eggs**, separated
175 g (6 oz) **caster sugar**
2 tablespoons **plain flour**,
   sifted
½ teaspoon **ground cinnamon**
2 tablespoons **warm water**
300 ml (½ pint) **double cream**
125 g (4 oz) **mini pink
   and white marshmallows**

Put the chocolate and butter in a bowl set over a saucepan of gently simmering water and leave to melt.

Whisk the egg whites in a large bowl until stiff, moist-looking peaks are formed, then gradually whisk in half the sugar, a teaspoonful at a time, until thick and glossy (see page 10). Using the still dirty whisk, beat the egg yolks and remaining sugar in a third bowl until very thick.

Mix the warm chocolate and butter mixture gradually into the egg yolks. Stir in the flour and cinnamon, then loosen the mixture with the measured warm water. Gently fold in a spoonful of the meringue, then fold in the remainder.

Pour the mixture into a greased and base-lined 23 cm (9 inch) springform tin. Bake in a preheated oven, 180°C (350°F), Gas Mark 4, for 25–30 minutes until well risen and the top is crusty and the centre only just set. Leave to cool for 2 hours in the tin.

Remove the torte from the tin, discarding the lining paper. Cut into wedges. Softly whip the cream, then top wedges of torte with spoonfuls of cream and a sprinkling of marshmallows.

For mixed nut torte, fold in 100 g (3½ oz) mixed pistachios, hazelnuts and almonds, roughly chopped, after the flour and cinnamon. Serve with 4 tablespoons toasted flaked almonds instead of the marshmallows.

topsy-turvy banana gingercake

Serves **6**
Preparation time **25 minutes**
Cooking time **30 minutes**

4 tablespoons **golden syrup**,
  plus extra to serve
4 tablespoons **light**
  muscovado sugar
3 large **bananas**, halved
  lengthways
juice of 1 **lemon**

Gingercake
100 g (3½ oz) **unsalted butter**
100 g (3½ oz) **light**
  muscovado sugar
75 g (3 oz) **golden syrup**,
  plus extra for drizzling
2 **eggs**
4 tablespoons **milk**
175 g (6 oz) **wholemeal**
  plain flour
1 teaspoon **bicarbonate**
  of soda
2 teaspoons **ground ginger**

Grease a roasting tin with a base measurement of 23 x 18 cm (9 x 7 inches), and line the base with nonstick baking paper. Spoon the syrup and sugar into the base. Toss the bananas in the lemon juice, then arrange cut side downwards in the tin.

Heat the butter, sugar and syrup for the gingercake gently in a medium saucepan, stirring until melted. Take the pan off the heat.

Beat the eggs and milk in a jug, then mix the flour, bicarbonate of soda and ginger in a bowl. Gradually stir the milk mixture into the pan of melted butter, then stir in the flour mix and beat until smooth.

Pour the mixture over the bananas, then bake them in a preheated oven, 180°C (350°F), Gas Mark 4, for 30 minutes until well risen and the centre springs back when pressed.

Leave to cool for 5 minutes, then loosen the edge and invert the tin on to a large plate with a rim. Remove the tin and lining paper, then cut the pudding into portions. Serve drizzled with a little extra syrup or custard.

For homemade custard, to serve with the gingercake, beat 3 egg yolks with 3 tablespoons caster sugar and a few drops vanilla essence in a bowl. In a pan bring 300 ml (½ pint) milk just to the boil, then gradually mix into the yolks. Return to the pan. Heat gently, stirring continuously until the custard thickens and coats the back of the spoon (don't boil or the custard will curdle). If making in advance, sprinkle the surface with a little extra sugar to stop a skin forming.

pear & hazelnut sponge squares

Serves **6**
Preparation time **25 minutes**
Cooking time **25 minutes**

125 g (4 oz) **unsalted butter**,
   at room temperature, or
   soft margarine
125 g (4 oz) **caster sugar**
125 g (4 oz) **self-raising flour**
2 **eggs**
1 teaspoon **ground cinnamon**
75 g (3 oz) **hazelnuts**, roughly
   chopped
3 **pears**, quartered, cored
   and peeled and each piece
   halved again
icing sugar, for dusting

Blackberry sauce
250 g (8 oz) **blackberries**
25 g (1 oz) **caster sugar**
4 tablespoons **water**

Beat the butter or margarine, sugar, flour, eggs and cinnamon together in a bowl or combine in a food processor until smooth. Stir in 50 g (2 oz) of the hazelnuts. Grease a roasting tin with a base measurement of 23 x 18 cm (9 x 7 inches) and line the base with nonstick baking paper. Spoon the mixture into the tin and smooth into an even layer.

Arrange the pears randomly over the pudding mix, then sprinkle with the remaining hazelnuts. Bake in a preheated oven, 180°C (350°F), Gas Mark 4, for 25 minutes until golden brown and the sponge is well risen and springs back when pressed in the centre.

Cook 150 g (5 oz) of the blackberries in a saucepan with the sugar and water for 5 minutes until soft, then purée until smooth. Cut the sponge into portions, dust with sifted icing sugar and serve drizzled with the warm sauce, with the remaining blackberries.

For apple squares with chocolate sauce, omit the cinnamon and hazelnuts from the sponge mix, adding the grated rind of ½ orange instead. Spoon into the tin, then top with 3 cored, peeled and thickly sliced dessert apples and bake as above. Heat 4 tablespoons chocolate and hazelnut spread in a saucepan with 6 tablespoons milk to make a smooth chocolate sauce. Cut the sponge into squares, dust with sifted icing sugar and serve hot with the sauce.

apricot clafouti

Serves **4**
Preparation time **15 minutes**,
  plus standing
Cooking time **25 minutes**

50 g (2 oz) **plain flour**
2 tablespoons **caster sugar**
grated rind of ½ **lemon**
40 g (1½ oz) **unsalted butter**
1 **egg**
1 **egg yolk**
few drops **vanilla essence**
150 ml (¼ pint) mixed **milk**
  and **water**
410 g (13½ oz) can **apricot
  halves**, drained
icing sugar, for dusting

Sift the flour into a bowl and add the sugar and lemon rind. Melt 25 g (1 oz) of the butter, then add to the flour with the whole egg, egg yolk and vanilla essence. Gradually whisk in the milk and water until smooth. Leave to stand for 30 minutes or longer.

Grease liberally 4 individual 200 ml (7 fl oz) metal pudding moulds with the remaining butter. Quarter the apricots and divide among the tins. Stand the tins on a baking sheet, then cook in a preheated oven, 190°C (375°F), Gas Mark 5, for 5 minutes.

Pour the batter quickly into the pudding moulds so that the mix sizzles in the hot butter. Bake for about 20 minutes until well risen and golden brown. Dust the tops with sifted icing sugar and serve immediately, as the puddings sink as they cool.

For cherry clafouti, make the batter with the grated rind of ½ orange instead of the lemon. Drain a 350 g (11 oz) jar of morello cherries in syrup and divide the cherries between the pudding moulds as above. Bake the fruit and then add the batter as above.

orchard fruit crumble

Serves **6**
Preparation time **20 minutes**
Cooking time **30–35 minutes**

2 **dessert apples**
2 **pears**
400 g (13 oz) **red plums,**
  quartered and pitted
2 tablespoons **water**
75 g (3 oz) **caster sugar**
100 g (3½ oz) **plain flour**
50 g (2 oz) **unsalted butter,**
  diced
50 g (2 oz) **desiccated**
  coconut
50 g (2 oz) **milk chocolate**
  chips

Quarter, core and peel the apples and pears. Slice the quarters and add the slices to a 1.2 litre (2 pint) pie dish. Add the plums and the water, then sprinkle with 25 g (1 oz) of the sugar. Cover the dish with foil and bake in a preheated oven, 180°C (350°F), Gas Mark 4, for 10 minutes.

Put the remaining sugar in a bowl with the flour and butter, then rub the butter in with your fingertips or an electric mixer until the mixture resembles fine crumbs. Stir in the coconut and chocolate chips.

Remove the foil from the fruit and spoon the crumble over the top. Bake for 20–25 minutes until golden brown and the fruit is tender. Serve warm with custard or cream.

For plum & orange crumble, put 750 g (1½ lb) plums, quartered and pitted, into a 1.2 litre (2 pint) pie dish with 50 g (2 oz) caster sugar. Make the crumble as above, adding the grated rind of 1 small orange and 50 g (2 oz) ground almonds instead of the coconut and chocolate chips. Bake as above.

red rice risotto & sautéed grapes

Serves **4**
Preparation time **15 minutes**
Cooking time **44–55 minutes**

75 g (3 oz) **unsalted butter**
175 g (6 oz) **Camargue red rice**, rinsed with cold water and drained
750–900 ml (1¼–1½ pints) **milk**
½ teaspoon **ground mixed spice**, plus a little extra to decorate
50 g (2 oz) **light muscovado sugar**
250 g (8 oz) **red seedless grapes**, halved
crème fraîche

Heat 50 g (2 oz) of the butter in a saucepan, add the rice and cook gently for 2 minutes, stirring. Heat the milk in a separate saucepan, pour about one-third over the rice and add the spice.

Cook the rice gently for 40–50 minutes, stirring occasionally until the rice is tender and creamy, topping up with ladlefuls of milk as the rice swells and stirring more frequently towards the end of the cooking time.

Take the rice off the heat and stir in the sugar. Heat the remaining butter in a frying pan, add the grapes and fry for 2–3 minutes until hot. Spoon the risotto into shallow bowls, top with spoonfuls of crème fraîche, then spoon the grapes and a little extra spice on top. Serve immediately.

For cherry risotto, fry 175 g (6 oz) white risotto rice in 50 g (2 oz) butter, then cook with 600–750 ml (1–1¼ pints) warmed milk as above, omitting the ground spice and adding 1 teaspoon vanilla essence and 50 g (2 oz) dried cherries instead. Simmer gently for 20–25 minutes until the rice is soft and creamy. Stir in 50 g (2 oz) caster sugar. Omit the grapes and top the risotto with spoonfuls of crème fraîche.

toffee & banana pancakes

Serves **4**
Preparation time **15 minutes**,
plus resting
Cooking time **30 minutes**

100 g (3½ oz) **plain flour**
pinch **salt**
1 **egg**
1 **egg yolk**
300 ml (½ pint) **milk**
2–3 tablespoons **sunflower oil**
2 **bananas**, sliced

Toffee sauce
50 g (2 oz) **unsalted butter**
50 g (2 oz) **light muscovado sugar**
2 tablespoons **golden syrup**
150 ml (¼ pint) **double cream**

Sift the flour into a bowl, add the salt, egg and egg yolk, then gradually whisk in the milk to make a smooth batter. Set aside for 30 minutes.

Put the butter, sugar and syrup for the toffee sauce in a small saucepan and heat gently, stirring occasionally, until the butter has melted and the sugar dissolved. Bring to the boil and cook for 3–4 minutes until just beginning to darken around the edges.

Take the pan off the heat, then gradually pour in the cream. Tilt the pan to mix and as bubbles subside stir with a wooden spoon. Set aside.

Pour the oil for cooking the pancakes into an 18 cm (7 inch) frying pan, heat and then pour off the excess into a small bowl or jug. Pour a little pancake batter over the base of the pan, tilt the pan to coat the base evenly with batter, then cook for 2 minutes until the underside is golden. Loosen with a palette knife, turn over and cook the second side in the same way. When cooked, slide on to a plate and keep hot. Cook the remaining batter, oiling the pan as needed.

Fold the pancakes and arrange on serving plates. Top with banana slices and drizzle with the toffee sauce.

For citrus pancakes, make the pancakes as above, then drizzle them with the freshly squeezed juice of 1 lemon and 1 orange. Sprinkle with 50 g (2 oz) caster sugar before serving.

cranberry eve's pudding

Serves **6**
Preparation time **25 minutes**
Cooking time **40–50 minutes**

750 g (1½ lb) **cooking
   apples**, quartered, cored,
   peeled and thickly sliced
125 g (4 oz) **frozen
   cranberries**
75 g (3 oz) **caster sugar**
1 tablespoon **water**
icing sugar, for dusting

Topping
125 g (4 oz) **unsalted butter**,
   at room temperature, or
   soft margarine
125 g (4 oz) **caster sugar**
125 g (4 oz) **self-raising flour**
2 **eggs**
grated rind of 1 small **orange**,
   plus 2 tablespoons of the
   juice

Put the apples and cranberries into a 1.5 litre (2½ pint), 5 cm (2 inch) deep ovenproof dish and sprinkle over the sugar and water. Cook, uncovered, in a preheated oven, 180°C (350°F), Gas Mark 4, for 10 minutes.

Put the butter, sugar, flour and eggs for the topping in a bowl, and beat together until smooth. Stir in the orange rind and juice.

Spoon the mixture over the partially cooked fruit and spread into an even layer. Return to the oven and cook for 30–40 minutes until the topping is golden and the centre springs back when pressed with a fingertip. Dust with sifted icing sugar and serve warm with custard or cream.

For apple & blackberry pudding, omit the cranberries and add 125 g (4 oz) frozen blackberries. Make the topping as above, but add the grated rind of 1 lemon and 2 tablespoons of the juice instead of the orange rind and juice.

pastries, pies & tarts

gingered profiteroles

Serves **4**
Preparation time **35 minutes**,
 plus cooling
Cooking time **20 minutes**

150 ml (¼ pint) **water**
50 g (2 oz) **unsalted butter**
pinch **salt**
65 g (2½ oz) **plain flour**, sifted
2 eggs
½ teaspoon **vanilla essence**
250 ml (8 fl oz) **double cream**
50 g (2 oz) **crystallized** or
 glacé ginger, finely chopped

Sauce
150 g (5 oz) **plain dark
 chocolate**, broken into
 pieces
150 ml (¼ pint) **milk**
50 g (2 oz) **caster sugar**
2 tablespoons **brandy**

Pour the measured water into a medium saucepan, add the butter and salt and heat until the butter has melted. Bring up to the boil, then take off the heat and stir in the flour. Put the pan back on the heat and cook briefly, stirring until the mixture makes a smooth ball. Leave to cool.

Beat the eggs and vanilla essence together, then gradually beat into the flour mixture until smooth. Spoon the mixture into a large piping bag fitted with a 1.5 cm (¾ inch) plain piping tube. Lightly grease a large baking sheet then pipe on 20 balls, leaving space between them.

Bake in a preheated oven, 200°C (400°F), Gas Mark 6, for 15 minutes until well risen. Make a slit in the side of each ball for the steam to escape, return to the turned-off oven for 5 minutes, then take out and cool.

Make the sauce by heating the chocolate, milk and sugar in a saucepan and stirring until smooth. Take off the heat and mix in the brandy.

Whip the cream until it forms soft swirls, fold in the ginger, then enlarge the slit in each profiterole and spoon in the ginger cream. Pile into serving dishes and drizzle with reheated sauce.

For Black Forest puffs, drain and chop a 425 g (14 oz) can of black cherries in juice. Fold into the whipped cream instead of the ginger, then fill the profiteroles as above. Omit the brandy from the sauce, adding 2 tablespoons kirsch instead.

macadamia & vanilla tart

Serves **8–10**
Preparation time **30 minutes**
Cooking time **45 minutes**

400 g (13 oz) chilled **ready-
made** or **homemade sweet
shortcrust pastry** (see
page 15)
a little **flour**, for dusting
75 g (3 oz) **light brown sugar**
150 ml (¼ pint) **maple syrup**
75 g (3 oz) **unsalted butter**
1 teaspoon **vanilla essence**
150 g (5 oz) **ground almonds**
4 **eggs**, beaten
200 g (7 oz) **macadamia
nuts**, coarsely chopped

Roll out the pastry thinly on a lightly floured surface
and line a 23 cm (9 inch) loose-bottomed baking
tin (see page 11). Prick the base, line with nonstick
baking paper, add macaroni or beans and bake blind
(see page 12) in a preheated oven, 190°C (375°F),
Gas Mark 5, for 15 minutes. Remove the paper and
macaroni or beans and bake for 5 minutes more.
Reduce the oven temperature to 160°C (325°F),
Gas Mark 3.

Heat the sugar, maple syrup and butter gently until
melted. Remove from the heat and beat in the vanilla
essence and ground almonds, followed by the eggs.
Add half the macadamia nuts and turn the mix into the
pastry shell.

Sprinkle with the remaining macadamia nuts and bake
for about 25 minutes or until the filling forms a crust
but remains quite soft underneath. Let the tart cool for
10 minutes, then serve with ice cream or cream.

For pine nut & honey tart, make and bake the tart
case as above. Cream together 100 g (3½ oz) unsalted
butter with 100 g (3½ oz) caster sugar. Beat in 3 eggs,
one at a time, then mix in 175 g (6 oz) warmed flower
honey, the grated rind and juice of 1 lemon and 200 g
(7 oz) pine nuts. Pour into the tart case and bake in
a preheated oven, 180°C (350°F), Gas Mark 4, for
about 40 minutes until browned and set.

peach & blueberry jalousie

Serves **6**
Preparation time **30 minutes**
Cooking time **20–25 minutes**

500 g (1 lb) chilled **ready-
made puff pastry** or
homemade flaky pastry
(see page 15)
a little **flour**, for dusting
4 ripe **peaches** or **nectarines**,
thickly sliced
125 g (4 oz) **blueberries**
50 g (2 oz) **caster sugar**, plus
a little extra to decorate
grated rind of ½ **lemon**
1 **egg**, beaten
icing sugar, for dusting

Roll out half the pastry on a lightly floured surface and trim to a 30 x 18 cm (12 x 7 inch) rectangle. Transfer to a lightly greased baking sheet.

Pile the peach or nectarine slices on top, leaving a 2.5 cm (1 inch) border of pastry showing, then sprinkle on the blueberries, sugar and lemon rind. Brush the pastry border with a little beaten egg.

Roll out the remaining pastry to a little larger than the first piece, then trim to 33 x 20 cm (13 x 8 inches). Fold in half lengthways, then make cuts in from the fold about 1 cm (½ inch) apart and about 6 cm (2½ inches) long, leaving a wide uncut border of pastry.

Lift the pastry over the fruit, unfold so that the fruit and bottom layer of pastry are completely covered, then press the pastry edges together. Trim if needed. Knock up the edges with a knife, then flute (see page 14).

Brush the top of the pastry with beaten egg, sprinkle with a little extra sugar and bake in a preheated oven, 200°C (400°F), Gas Mark 6, for 20–25 minutes until the pastry is well risen and golden brown. Serve cut into squares, warm or cold, with cream or ice cream.

For apple & blackberry jalousie, replace the peaches and blueberries with 4 Granny Smith apples, cored, quartered and thickly sliced, and 125 g (4 oz) blackberries.

strawberry choux puffs

Makes **12**
Preparation time **30 minutes**
Cooking time **30 minutes**

50 g (2 oz) **unsalted butter**,
  cut into pieces
150 ml (¼ pint) **water**
65 g (2½ oz) **plain flour**, sifted
2 **eggs**, beaten
1 teaspoon **vanilla extract**
325 g (11 oz) **strawberries**,
  thinly sliced
icing sugar, for dusting

Crème pâtissière
1 **vanilla pod**
150 ml (¼ pint) **milk**
150 ml (¼ pint) **double cream**
4 **egg yolks**
3 tablespoons **caster sugar**
2 tablespoons **plain flour**

Grease a large baking sheet lightly and sprinkle with water. Melt the butter in a medium saucepan with the water. Bring to the boil, then remove from the heat.

Add the sifted flour and beat until the mix forms a ball. Allow to cool for 15 minutes, then gradually beat in the eggs until smooth and glossy. Add the vanilla essence.

Place 12 equal spoonfuls of the mix, spaced well apart, on the sheet and bake in a preheated oven, 200°C (400°F), Gas Mark 6, for 25 minutes or until well risen and golden. Slit around the middle of each and return to the oven for 3 minutes. Transfer to a rack to cool.

Make the crème pâtissière. Slit the vanilla pod and scrape out the seeds. Put milk and double cream in a pan and add the seeds and pod. Bring almost to the boil, then leave to stand for 20 minutes. Beat together the yolks, caster sugar and plain flour. Remove the vanilla pod, reheat the milk mixture, then gradually whisk into the yolks. Pour back into the pan and cook gently for 4–5 minutes, stirring until very thick. Turn into a bowl, cover the surface with clingfilm and leave to cool.

Open out each puff and divide the sliced strawberries among them. Pile the crème pâtissière on top and push the puffs back together so the strawberries and crème pâtissière still show around the centre. Dust with icing sugar and store in a cool place until ready to serve.

For lemon & peach buns, whip 150 ml (½ pint) double cream until it forms soft swirls. Fold in 150 g (5 oz) Greek yogurt and 3 tablespoons lemon curd. Fill each baked puff with 2 thinly sliced ripe peaches and spoonfuls of the lemon cream. Dust with icing sugar.

pear dumplings with figs

Serves **6**
Preparation time **40 minutes**
Cooking time **15–20 minutes**

125 g (4 oz) ready-to-eat
   dried figs, finely chopped
grated rind and juice of
   1 large **orange**
6 firm, ripe **pears**
500 g (1 lb) chilled **ready-
   made puff pastry** or
   homemade flaky pastry
   (see page 15)
a little **flour**, for dusting
1 **egg**, beaten
icing sugar, for dusting

Put the figs in a small saucepan with the orange rind
and juice. Cover and simmer gently for 5 minutes until
soft, adding a little extra water if needed. Leave to cool.

Peel the pears and take out the cores via the bases.
Trim off the bases so that they stand upright, then
spoon the fig mixture into the core cavity and press
down firmly.

Roll the pastry out thinly on a lightly floured surface
and trim to a 43 x 38 cm (17 x 15 inch) rectangle.
Cut a 6 cm (2½ inch) wide strip off one of the long
sides, then cut the strip into 6 small squares. Place
each square under the base of the pear to stop the
stuffing coming out.

Brush the remaining pastry with beaten egg, then cut
into long thin strips about 2.5 cm (1 inch) wide. Take
the strips one at a time and wind around each pear,
beginning at the top and curling around the pear, with
the strip slightly overlapping, until the base is reached.
Add a second strip if needed.

Put the dumplings on a greased baking sheet and
cook in a preheated oven, 200°C (400°F), Gas Mark 6,
for 15–20 minutes until golden brown. Dust with sifted
icing sugar and serve hot with custard.

For Christmas gingered pear dumplings, combine
3 tablespoons luxury fruit mincemeat with 15 g (½ oz)
finely chopped crystallized or glacé ginger. Spoon the
mixture into 6 peeled, cored pears. Wrap in pastry and
cook as above. Serve with crème fraîche mixed with a
little brandy or whisky.

freeform apple & mixed berry pie

Serves **6**

Preparation time **30 minutes**,
  plus chilling

Cooking time **20–25 minutes**

275 g (9 oz) **plain flour**, plus
  extra for dusting

75 g (3 oz) **icing sugar**

125 g (4 oz) **unsalted butter**,
  at room temperature, diced

2 **eggs**

a little **milk** or beaten **egg**,
  to glaze

caster sugar, to decorate

Filling

2 **cooking apples**, about
  500 g (1 lb), cored, peeled
  and thickly sliced

175 g (6 oz) **frozen mixed
  berries** (no need to defrost)

50 g (2 oz) **icing sugar**

2 teaspoons **cornflour**

Put the flour on a large board or straight on to the work surface, add the icing sugar and butter, then make a dip in the centre and add the eggs. Begin to mix the eggs and butter together with your fingertips, gradually drawing the flour and sugar into the mix until it begins to clump together and you can squeeze the pastry into a ball. Knead the pastry lightly, then chill in the refrigerator for 15 minutes.

Mix together the apples, frozen mixed berries, icing sugar and cornflour for the filling.

Roll out the pastry on a lightly floured surface until it forms a rough-shaped circle about 33 cm (13 inches) in diameter. Lift it over a rolling pin on to a large greased baking sheet. Pile the fruit mix high in the centre of the pastry, then bring the edges of the pastry up and around the fruit, shaping into soft pleats and leaving the centre of the fruit mound exposed.

Brush the outside of the pie with a little milk or beaten egg and sprinkle with caster sugar. Bake in a preheated oven, 190°C (375°F), Gas Mark 5, for 20–25 minutes until the pastry is golden and the fruit tender. Serve warm or cold with custard or cream.

For spiced plum & peach pie, replace the apples and berries with 400 g (13 oz) ripe red plums, pitted and sliced, and 2 ripe peaches, sliced. Mix with the sugar and cornflour as above, adding ½ teaspoon ground cinnamon. Make the pie and bake as above.

portuguese custard tarts

Makes **12**
Preparation time **25 minutes**,
  plus cooling
Cooking time **35 minutes**

1 tablespoon **vanilla sugar**
½ teaspoon **ground cinnamon**
450 g (14½ oz) chilled **ready-
  made** or **homemade sweet
  shortcrust pastry** (see
  page 15)
a little **flour**, for dusting
3 **eggs**
2 **egg yolks**
2 tablespoons **caster sugar**
1 teaspoon **vanilla essence**
300 ml (½ pint) **double cream**
150 ml (¼ pint) **milk**
icing sugar, for dusting

Mix the vanilla sugar with the cinnamon. Cut the pastry in half and roll out each piece on a lightly floured surface to a 20 cm (8 inch) square. Sprinkle 1 square with the spiced sugar and position the second square on top. Reroll the pastry to a 40 x 30 cm (16 x 12 inch) rectangle and cut out 12 circles, each 10 cm (4 inch) across, using a large cutter or small bowl as a guide.

Press the pastry circles into the sections of a 12-hole nonstick muffin tray, pressing them firmly into the bottom and around the sides. Prick each pastry base, line with a square of foil, add macaroni or beans and bake blind (see page 12) in a preheated oven, 190°C (375°F), Gas Mark 5, for 10 minutes. Remove the foil and macaroni or beans and bake for an additional 5 minutes. Reduce the oven temperature to 160°C (325°F), Gas Mark 3.

Beat together the eggs, egg yolks, caster sugar and vanilla essence. Heat the cream and milk in a pan until bubbling around the edges and pour it over the egg mixture, stirring. Strain the custard into a jug and pour into the pastry shells.

Bake for about 20 minutes or until the custard is only just set. Let the tarts cool in the tin, then remove and serve dusted with icing sugar.

For French prune custard tarts, put 12 ready-to-eat pitted prunes in the base of each blind-baked pastry case, then pour the custard over and bake as above. Serve warm with spoonfuls of crème fraîche.

lemon meringue pie

Serves **6**
Preparation time **40 minutes**,
  plus chilling and standing
Cooking time **35–40 minutes**

375 g (12 oz) chilled **ready-
  made** or **homemade sweet
  shortcrust pastry** (see
  page 15)
a little **flour**, for dusting
200 g (7 oz) **caster sugar**
40 g (1½ oz) **cornflour**
grated rind and juice of
  2 **lemons**
4 **eggs**, separated
200–250 ml (7–8 fl oz) **water**

Roll out the pastry thinly on a lightly floured surface and use to line a 20 cm (8 inch) diameter x 5 cm (2 inch) deep loose-bottomed fluted flan tin, pressing evenly into the sides (see page 11). Trim the top and prick the base. Chill for 15 minutes, then line with nonstick baking paper, add macaroni or beans and bake blind (see page 12) in a preheated oven, 190°C (375°F), Gas Mark 5, for 15 minutes. Remove the paper and macaroni or beans and bake for 5 more minutes.

Put 75 g (3 oz) of the sugar in a bowl with the cornflour and lemon rind, add the egg yolks and mix until smooth. Make the lemon juice up to 300 ml (½ pint) with water, pour into a saucepan and bring to the boil. Gradually mix into the yolk mixture, whisking until smooth. Pour back into the pan and bring to the boil, whisking until very thick. Pour into the pastry case and spread level.

Whisk the egg whites until they form stiff peaks. Gradually whisk in the remaining sugar, a teaspoonful at a time, then whisk for 1–2 minutes more until thick and glossy (see page 10). Spoon over the lemon layer to cover completely and swirl with a spoon.

Reduce the oven to 180°C (350°F), Gas Mark 4, and cook for 15–20 minutes until the meringue is golden and cooked through. Leave to stand for 15 minutes, then remove the tart tin and transfer to a serving plate. Serve warm or cold with cream.

For citrus meringue pie, mix the grated rind of 1 lime, 1 lemon and ½ small orange with the cornflour. Squeeze the juice from the fruits and make up to 300 ml (½ pint) with water. Continue as above.

classic lemon tart

Serves **8**

Preparation time **20 minutes**,
plus chilling and cooling

Cooking time **45–50 minutes**

450 g (14½ oz) chilled **ready-
made** or **homemade sweet
shortcrust pastry** (see
page 15)

3 **eggs**

1 **egg yolk**

450 ml (¾ pint) **double cream**

100 g (3½ oz) **caster sugar**

150 ml (¼ pint) **lemon juice**

icing sugar, for dusting

Roll out pastry thinly on a lightly floured surface and
use it to line a 25 cm (10 inch) fluted flan tin (see
page 11). Prick the pastry shell with a fork and then
chill for 15 minutes.

Line the pastry shell with nonstick baking paper, add
macaroni or beans and bake blind (see page 12) in
a preheated oven, 190°C (375°F), Gas Mark 5, for
15 minutes. Remove the paper and macaroni or
beans and bake for a further 10 minutes until crisp
and golden. Remove from the oven and reduce the
temperature to 150°C (300°F), Gas Mark 2.

Beat together the eggs, egg yolk, double cream, sugar
and lemon juice, then pour into the pastry shell.

Bake for 20–25 minutes or until the filling is just set.
Let the tart cool completely, then dust with icing sugar
and serve.

For mixed berries with cassis, to serve with the tart,
halve or slice 250 g (8 oz) strawberries, depending
on their size, and mix with 125 g (4 oz) raspberries,
125 g (4 oz) blueberries, 3 tablespoons caster sugar
and 2 tablespoons crème de cassis. Soak for 1 hour
before serving.

gateau pithiviers with plums

Serves **6**
Preparation time **30 minutes**
Cooking time **25–30 minutes**

100 g (3½ oz) **unsalted
butter**, at room temperature
100 g (3½ oz) **caster sugar**
100 g (3½ oz) **ground
almonds**
few drops **almond essence**
1 **egg**, beaten, plus extra for
glazing
500 g (1 lb) chilled **ready-
made puff pastry** or
homemade flaky pastry
(see page 15)
a little **flour**, for dusting
375 g (12 oz) **plums**, pitted
and thickly sliced
icing sugar, for dusting

Cream the butter and sugar together in a bowl until pale and smooth. Add the almonds and almond essence, then the egg, and mix together until smooth.

Roll out half the pastry thinly on a lightly floured surface and trim to a 25 cm (10 inch) circle using a dinner plate as a guide. Place on a wetted baking sheet, then spread the almond paste over the top leaving a 2.5 cm (1 inch) border of pastry around the edges. Arrange the plums in a single layer on top. Brush the pastry border with a little beaten egg.

Roll out the remaining pastry thinly and trim to a circle a little larger than the first. Cut 5 or 6 swirly 'S' shapes out of the centre of the pastry, then lift over a rolling pin and position on the almond paste. Press the edges together to seal, and trim to neaten if needed. Knock up the edge to separate the pastry layers slightly, then flute the edge (see page 14).

Brush the top with beaten egg and bake in a preheated oven, 200°C (400°F), Gas Mark 6, for 25–30 minutes until well risen and golden.

Leave to cool slightly, then dust the top with icing sugar and serve cut into wedges with cream.

For brandied prune Pithiviers, soak 150 g (5 oz) ready-to-eat pitted prunes in 3 tablespoons brandy, then arrange over the almond paste instead of the plums. Continue as above.

pecan, maple syrup & choc tart

Serves **8**
Preparation time **20 minutes**,
 plus chilling and cooling
Cooking time **1 hour–1 hour
 10 minutes**

175 g (6 oz) **plain flour**,
 sifted, plus extra for dusting
25 g (1 oz) **cocoa powder**,
 sifted
¼ teaspoon **salt**
100 g (3½ oz) chilled **unsalted
 butter**, diced
1 **egg**, lightly beaten
2–3 teaspoons **cold water**

Filling
125 g (4 oz) **unsalted butter**,
 softened
125 g (4 oz) **light soft brown
 sugar**
2 **eggs**, beaten
4 tablespoons **plain flour**
pinch **salt**
175 ml (6 fl oz) **maple syrup**
175 g (6 oz) **pecan nuts**,
 toasted
100 g (3½ oz) **pine nuts**,
 lightly toasted
50 g (2 oz) **plain dark
 chocolate**, chopped

Place the flour, cocoa powder and salt in a bowl, add the butter and rub in with the fingertips until the mixture resembles fine breadcrumbs. Add the egg and water and continue mixing until the pastry just starts to come together. Transfer to a lightly floured surface, knead gently and form into a flat disc. Wrap the dough in clingfilm and chill for 30 minutes.

Roll out the dough thinly on a lightly floured surface and use it to line a 23 cm (9 inch) square flan tin (see page 11). Prick the base and chill for 20 minutes. Line the tin with nonstick baking paper, add macaroni or beans and bake blind (see page 12) in a preheated oven, 190°C (375°F), Gas Mark 5, for 15 minutes. Remove the paper and beans or macaroni and bake for a further 5–10 minutes or until crisp and golden. Leave to cool. Reduce the temperature to 180°C (350°F), Gas Mark 4.

Cream the butter and sugar until pale and light, then gradually beat in the eggs, adding the flour and salt as you go until evenly combined. Stir in the syrup (the mixture may appear to curdle at this stage), nuts and chocolate and spoon the mixture into the pastry case.

Bake for 40–45 minutes until golden and just firm in the centre. Remove from the oven and leave to cool. Serve warm with double cream.

For traditional pecan pie, replace the cocoa with an extra 25 g (1 oz) plain flour and a large pinch of ground mixed spice in the pastry. Use 250 g (8 oz) pecan nuts and omit the pine nuts and chocolate, flavouring with 1 teaspoon vanilla essence instead.

cherry frangipane tart

Serves **8**

Preparation time **35 minutes**, plus chilling and cooling

Cooking time **50 minutes**

450 g (14½ oz) chilled **ready-made** or **homemade sweet shortcrust pastry** (see page 15)

a little **flour**, for dusting

250 g (8 oz) **fresh cherries**, pitted, or a 425 g (14 oz) can, drained

3 **eggs**

100 g (3½ oz) **caster sugar**

75 g (3 oz) **unsalted butter**, melted

few drops **almond essence**

100 g (3½ oz) **ground almonds**

2 tablespoons **flaked almonds**

icing sugar, for dusting

Roll out the pastry on a lightly floured surface until large enough to line a 25 cm (10 inch) greased deep-fluted, loose-bottomed flan tin (see page 11). Lift the pastry over a rolling pin, then press it over the base and sides of the tin. Trim the top, then chill for 15 minutes.

Prick the base of the tart with a fork. Line the pastry with nonstick baking paper, add macaroni or beans and bake blind (see page 12) in a preheated oven, 190°C (375°F), Gas Mark 5, for 15 minutes. Remove the paper and macaroni or beans and cook for a further 5 minutes.

Arrange the cherries in the base of the tart. Whisk the eggs and sugar together until thick and the whisk leaves a trail when lifted out of the mixture. Gently fold in the melted butter and almond essence, then the ground almonds. Pour the mixture over the cherries and sprinkle with the flaked almonds.

Reduce the oven to 180°C (350°F), Gas Mark 4, and cook the tart for 30 minutes until golden brown and the filling is set. Check after 20 minutes and cover the top loosely with foil if the tart appears to be browning too quickly.

Leave to cool in the tin for 30 minutes, then remove and dust with sifted icing sugar before serving.

For Bakewell tart, make the tart case and bake blind as above, then spread 4 tablespoons strawberry or raspberry jam over the base. Add the almond mixture and flaked almonds and bake as above.

pear & almond tart

Serves **8**

Preparation time **20 minutes**, plus chilling

Cooking time **50–55 minutes**

450 g (14½ oz) chilled **ready-made** or **homemade sweet shortcrust pastry** (see page 15)

a little **flour**, for dusting

125 g (4 oz) **unsalted butter**, softened

125 g (4 oz) **caster sugar**

125 g (4 oz) **ground almonds**

2 **eggs**, lightly beaten

1 tablespoon **lemon juice**

3 ripe **pears**, peeled, cored and thickly sliced

25 g (1 oz) **flaked almonds**

icing sugar, for dusting

Roll out the pastry on a lightly floured surface and use it to line a 25 cm (10 inch) flan tin (see page 11). Prick the base with a fork and chill for 30 minutes. Line with nonstick baking paper, add macaroni or beans and bake blind (see page 12) in a preheated oven, 190°C (375°F), Gas Mark 5, for 15 minutes. Remove the baking paper and macaroni or beans and bake for a further 5–10 minutes until the pastry is crisp and golden. Leave to cool completely. Reduce the temperature to 190°C (375°F), Gas Mark 5.

Beat the butter, sugar and ground almonds together until smooth, then beat in the eggs and lemon juice.

Arrange the pear slices over the pastry case and carefully spread over the almond mixture. Sprinkle with the flaked almonds and bake for 30 minutes until the topping is golden and firm to the touch. Remove from the oven and leave to cool.

Dust the tart with sifted icing sugar and serve in wedges with chocolate sauce (see below) and some vanilla ice cream.

For chocolate sauce, to serve as an accompaniment, melt 100 g (3½ oz) plain dark chocolate, chopped, 50 g (2 oz) unsalted butter, diced, and 1 tablespoon golden syrup together. Leave to cool slightly.

sweet fruity pizzas

Serves **4**
Preparation time **25 minutes**,
  plus rising
Cooking time **12–15 minutes**

250 g (8 oz) **strong white
  flour**, plus extra for dusting
¼ teaspoon **salt**
2 tablespoons **caster sugar**
¾ teaspoon **fast-action dried
  yeast**
2 tablespoons **olive oil**
150 ml (¼ pint) **warm water**

Topping
150 g (5 oz) **full-fat
  mascarpone cheese**
2 tablespoons **icing sugar**
½ teaspoon **vanilla essence**
2 **peaches**, pitted and sliced
2 **figs**, quartered
125 g (4 oz) **fresh
  raspberries**
2 tablespoons **maple syrup**,
  plus extra to serve

Put the flour, salt, sugar and yeast in a bowl and mix together. Add the oil, then gradually stir in the measured warm water and mix to a smooth dough. Knead on a lightly floured surface for 5 minutes until smooth and elastic. Put back in the bowl, cover with greased clingfilm and leave in a warm place for about 45 minutes until doubled in size.

Knead the dough for a second time, then roll out to 4 rough-shaped circles about 18 cm (7 inches) in diameter. Place on 2 greased baking sheets.

Mix the mascarpone with the icing sugar and vanilla essence, then spread over the pizzas leaving a rim of dough. Arrange the fruit on top. Leave to rise for 15 minutes. Drizzle with the maple syrup, then bake in a preheated oven, 200°C (400°F), Gas Mark 6, for 12–15 minutes until the pizzas are golden and the bread bases cooked through.

Leave to stand for 5 minutes, drizzle with a little extra maple syrup, then serve.

For marzipan & nectarine fruit kuchen, add the grated rind of 1 lemon when mixing the bread dough, knead, leave to rise and knead again as above, then press into a 25 cm (10 inch) greased fluted, loose-bottomed flan tin. Sprinkle with 75 g (3 oz) grated marzipan, then arrange 2 sliced nectarines over the top. Drizzle with 2 tablespoons melted butter and 2 tablespoons caster sugar. Leave to rise, then bake for 25–30 minutes at the temperature given above, covering with foil after 15 minutes if overbrowning.

mixed berry tartlets

Serves **6**
Preparation time **20 minutes**,
  plus chilling
Cooking time **40–48 minutes**

450 g (14½ oz) chilled **ready-
  made** or **homemade sweet
  shortcrust pastry** (see
  page 15)
a little **flour**, for dusting
icing sugar, for dusting

Filling
125 g (4 oz) **unsalted butter**,
  softened
125 g (4 oz) **caster sugar**
2 **eggs**, lightly beaten
125 g (4 oz) **ground
  hazelnuts**
175 g (6 oz) **mixed summer
  berries** (such as raspberries
  and blueberries)

Apricot glaze
250 g (8 oz) **apricot jam**
2 teaspoons **lemon juice**
2 teaspoons **water**

Divide the pastry into 3 pieces and roll each one out thinly on a lightly floured surface. Use to line 3 x 12 cm (5 inch) fluted flan tins (see page 11). Prick the bases with a fork and chill for 30 minutes. Line with nonstick baking paper, add macaroni or beans and bake blind (see page 12) in a preheated oven, 190°C (375°F), Gas Mark 5, for 10 minutes. Remove the paper and macaroni or beans and bake for a further 5–8 minutes until crisp and golden. Leave to cool. Reduce the temperature to 180°C (350°F), Gas Mark 4.

Beat the butter and sugar until pale and light, then gradually beat in the eggs. Fold in the hazelnuts.

Divide the berries among the pastry cases and spoon over the hazelnut mixture, spreading it flat. Bake for 25–30 minutes or until risen and firm to the touch.

Put the jam in a small pan with the lemon juice and measured water and heat gently until the jam melts. Increase the heat and boil for 1 minute, remove from the heat and press through a fine sieve. Keep warm.

Brush the warm apricot glaze brush over the tarts as soon as they come out of the oven. Leave to cool in the tins and serve dusted with icing sugar.

For raspberry & almondine tart, line a 20 cm (8 inch) flan tin with pastry and bake blind as above. Sprinkle over 175 g (6 oz) fresh raspberries. Cream the butter and sugar as above, then beat in the eggs, 125 g (4 oz) ground almonds and a few drops almond essence. Spoon into the case and sprinkle with 3 tablespoons flaked almonds. Bake as above for 35–45 minutes.

deep dish puff apple pie

Serves **6**
Preparation time **40 minutes**,
    plus chilling
Cooking time **20–25 minutes**

1 kg (2 lb) or about 5 **cooking
    apples**, quartered, cored,
    peeled and thickly sliced
100 g (3½ oz) **caster sugar**,
    plus extra for sprinkling
grated rind of 1 small **orange**
½ teaspoon **ground mixed
    spice** or **ground cinnamon**
3 whole **cloves**
400 g (13 oz) chilled **ready-
    made puff pastry** or
    homemade flaky pastry
    (see page 15)
a little **flour**, for dusting
1 **egg**, beaten

Fill a 1.2 litre (2 pint) pie dish with the apples. Mix
the sugar with the orange rind, mixed spice and cloves,
then sprinkle over the apples.

Roll the pastry out on a lightly floured surface until a
little larger than the top of the dish. Cut 2 long strips
from the edges, about 1 cm (½ inch) wide. Brush the
dish rim with a little beaten egg, press the strips on top,
then brush these with egg (see pages 13–14). Lift the
remaining pastry over the dish and press the edges
together well.

Trim off the excess pastry, knock up the edges with a
small knife, then flute. Reroll the trimmings and cut out
small heart shapes or circles with a small biscuit cutter.
Brush the top of the pie with beaten egg, add pastry
shapes, then brush these with egg. Sprinkle with a little
extra sugar.

Bake in a preheated oven, 200°C (400°F), Gas Mark
6, for 20–25 minutes until the pastry is well risen and
golden. Serve warm with spoonfuls of crème fraîche or
extra-thick cream.

For spiced plum & pear pie, substitute 500 g (1 lb)
sliced pears and 500 g (1 lb) sliced plums for the
apples, sprinkle with 75 g (3 oz) caster sugar and add
2 halved star anise, 3 cloves and ¼ teaspoon ground
cinnamon. Omit the fruit rind, then cover with the
pastry and continue as above.

mango & palm sugar tatin

Serves **8**

Preparation time **40 minutes**, plus freezing

Cooking time **20–25 minutes**

75 g (3 oz) **unsalted butter**

75 g (3 oz) **palm sugar**, grated, or **light soft brown sugar**

½ teaspoon ground **mixed spice**

3 small **mangoes**, peeled, pitted and thickly sliced

350 g (12 oz) chilled **ready-made puff pastry** or **homemade flaky pastry** (see page 15)

a little **flour**, for dusting

Make the topping. Heat the butter, sugar and spice together in a 23 cm (9 inch) ovenproof frying pan until the butter has melted. Remove the pan from the heat. Carefully arrange the mango slices in the pan, fanning them from the centre outwards, to make 2 layers.

Roll out the pastry on a lightly floured surface and trim to a round a little larger than the size of the pan. Press it down over the mangoes and into the edges of the pan and pierce a small hole in the centre. Bake in a preheated oven, 220°C (425°F), Gas Mark 7, for 20–25 minutes until the pastry is risen and golden. Leave to stand for 10 minutes before turning out on to a large plate. Serve with ice cream.

For coconut ice cream, to accompany the tatin, bring 300 ml (½ pint) full-fat milk, 400 ml (14 fl oz) can full-fat coconut milk and 2 star anise just to the boil in a saucepan. Take off the heat and leave to infuse for 20 minutes, then strain. Beat 5 egg yolks with 75 g (3 oz) caster sugar until pale and creamy. Stir in the cream mix, then pour back into the pan and heat gently, stirring until it coats the back of the spoon. Cool, then freeze in an electric ice-cream machine until thick or in a plastic box in the freezer, beating several times until firm.

pumpkin pie

Serves **6**
Preparation time **30 minutes**
Cooking time **60–75 minutes**

500 g (1 lb) **pumpkin** or
   butternut squash, weighed
   after deseeding and peeling
3 **eggs**
100 g (3½ oz) **light
   muscovado sugar**
2 tablespoons **plain flour**
½ teaspoon **ground cinnamon**
½ teaspoon **ground ginger**
¼ teaspoon **grated nutmeg**
200 ml (7 fl oz) **milk**, plus
   extra for glazing
450 g (14½ oz) chilled **ready-
   made** or **homemade sweet
   shortcrust pastry** (see
   page 15)
a little **flour**, for dusting
icing sugar, for dusting

Cut the pumpkin or butternut squash into cubes and cook in a covered steamer for 15–20 minutes, until tender. Cool, then purée in a liquidizer or food processor.

Whisk the eggs, sugar, flour and spices together in a bowl until just mixed. Add the pumpkin purée, whisk together, then gradually mix in the milk. Set aside.

Roll out three-quarters of the pastry on a lightly floured surface until large enough to line a greased 23 cm (9 inch) x 2.5 cm (1 inch) deep enamel pie dish. Lift the pastry over the rolling pin and press over the base and sides of the dish. Trim off the excess around the rim and add the trimmings to the reserved pastry. Roll out thinly and cut leaves, then mark veins. Brush the rim of the pastry in the dish, then press on the leaves, reserving a few. Stand the dish on a baking sheet.

Pour the pumpkin filling into the dish, add a few leaves if liked on top of the filling, then brush these and the dish edges lightly with milk. Bake in a preheated oven, 190°C (375°F), Gas Mark 5, for 45–55 minutes until the filling is set and the pastry cooked through. Cover with foil after 20 minutes to stop the pastry edge from overbrowning.

Serve dusted with a little icing sugar, with whipped cream sprinkled with a little extra ground spice, if liked.

For gingered pumpkin pie with maple syrup, omit the muscovado sugar and add 6 tablespoons maple syrup. Omit the ground cinnamon and nutmeg and increase the ground ginger to 1½ teaspoons, adding 2 tablespoons finely chopped glacé or stem ginger.

kaffir lime tart

Serves **8**
Preparation time **20 minutes**,
  plus chilling
Cooking time **33–40 minutes**

400 g (13 oz) chilled **ready-
  made** or **homemade sweet
  shortcrust pastry** (see
  page 15)
a little **flour**, for dusting
175 g (6 oz) **caster sugar**
200 ml (7 fl oz) freshly
  squeezed **lime juice**
  (4–6 limes)
8 **kaffir lime leaves** or the
  grated rind of 3 **limes**
3 **eggs**
2 **egg yolks**
175 g (6 oz) **unsalted butter**,
  softened
icing sugar, for dusting

Roll out the pastry on a lightly floured surface and use it to line a 23 cm (9 inch) flan tin (see page 11). Prick the base with a fork and chill for 30 minutes. Line with nonstick baking paper, add macaroni or beans and bake blind (see page 12) in a preheated oven, 200°C (400°F), Gas Mark 6, for 15 minutes. Remove the paper and macaroni or beans and bake for a further 12–15 minutes until the pastry is crisp and golden. Set aside to cool.

Make the filling. Put the sugar, lime juice and kaffir lime leaves or lime rind in a saucepan and heat gently to dissolve the sugar. Bring to the boil and simmer for 5 minutes. Leave to cool for 5 minutes, then strain into a clean pan.

Stir in the eggs, egg yolks and half the butter and heat gently, stirring, for 1 minute or until the sauce coats the back of the spoon. Add the remaining butter and whisk constantly until the mixture thickens.

Transfer the lime mixture to the pastry case and bake for 6–8 minutes until set. Leave to cool and serve warm dusted with icing sugar.

For mango & kiwifruit salad, to serve with the tart, peel, stone and dice 1 large mango, then mix with 3 peeled and sliced kiwifruits, the seeds scooped from 3 passion fruits and the juice of 1 lime.

plum tripiti

Makes **24**
Preparation time **40 minutes**
Cooking time **10 minutes**

100 g (3½ oz) **feta cheese**,
    drained and coarsely grated
100 g (3½ oz) **ricotta cheese**
50 g (2 oz) **caster sugar**
¼ teaspoon **ground cinnamon**
1 **egg**, beaten
75 g (3 oz) **unsalted butter**
12 sheets chilled **filo pastry**
    from a 200 g (7 oz) pack
a little **flour**, for dusting
500 g (1 lb) small red **plums**,
    halved and pitted
icing sugar, for dusting

Mix the feta, ricotta, sugar, cinnamon and egg in a bowl. Melt the butter in a small saucepan.

Unfold the pastry sheets on a lightly floured surface, then put one in front of you, with a short side facing you. Cover the remaining sheets with clingfilm to prevent them drying out. Brush the pastry sheet with a little of the melted butter, then cut in half to make two long strips. Place a spoonful of the cheese mixture a little up from the bottom left-hand corner of each strip, then cover with a plum half. Fold the bottom right-hand corner of one strip diagonally over the plum to cover the filling and to make a triangle.

Fold the bottom left-hand corner upwards to make a second triangle, then keep folding until the top of the strip is reached and the filling is enclosed in a triangle of pastry. Place on a baking sheet and repeat until 24 triangles have been made using all the filling.

Brush the outside of the triangles with the remaining butter and cook in a preheated oven, 200°C (400°F), Gas Mark 6, for about 10 minutes until the pastry is golden and the plum juices begin to run from the sides. Dust with a little sifted icing sugar and leave to cool for 15 minutes before serving.

For gingered peach tripiti, make the filling in the same way but flavour with 2 tablespoons finely chopped glacé or stem ginger instead of ground cinnamon. Top with 2 ripe peaches, each cut into 12 pieces.

apple & muscatel strudel

Serves **6**
Preparation time **30 minutes**,
  plus soaking
Cooking time **30–35 minutes**

100 g (3½ oz) **muscatel
  raisins**
2 tablespoons **brandy**
750 g (1½ lb) **dessert apples**,
  quartered, cored and cut into
  small dice
75 g (3 oz) **fresh white
  breadcrumbs**
50 g (2 oz) **soft light brown
  sugar**
grated rind of 1 **lemon**
50 g (2 oz) **pine nuts**, toasted
1 teaspoon **ground
  cinnamon**, plus extra for
  dusting
12 sheets chilled **filo pastry**
  from a 200 g (7 oz) pack
a little **flour**, for dusting
65 g (2½ oz) **unsalted butter**,
  melted
2 tablespoons **icing sugar**,
  for dusting

Put the raisins in a bowl and cover with the brandy.
Set aside to soak for 2 hours.

Put the apples in a bowl and add the breadcrumbs,
sugar, lemon rind, pine nuts, cinnamon and the raisins
and their juices. Stir well.

Lay 2 sheets of the pastry on a lightly floured work
surface, next to each other and overlapping by about
2.5 cm (1 inch) to form a larger sheet of pastry. Brush
with melted butter, then top with the remaining pastry,
brushing each layer with a little butter.

Spread the apple mixture over the pastry, leaving a
5 cm (2 inch) border. Fold the long sides over the
filling. Brush with butter and roll up from a short side
to form a Swiss roll.

Transfer to a baking sheet, brush with the remaining
melted butter and bake in a preheated oven, 200°C
(400°F), Gas Mark 6, for 30–35 minutes until lightly
golden. Combine the sifted icing sugar with a little
extra cinnamon and dust the strudel. Serve hot with
custard or whipped cream.

For plum & almond strudel, omit the raisins, brandy
and apples and mix 625 g (1¼ lb) pitted and thickly
sliced red plums with the breadcrumbs, sugar, lemon
rind, 50 g (2 oz) ground almonds and 1 teaspoon
ground cinnamon. Continue as above.

double chocolate tart

Serves **6–8**

Preparation time **40 minutes**, plus chilling and cooling

Cooking time **40 minutes**

400 g (13 oz) chilled **ready-made** or **homemade sweet shortcrust pastry** (see page 15)

a little **flour**, for dusting

150 g (5 oz) **plain dark chocolate**, broken into pieces, plus 50 g (2 oz) to decorate

150 g (5 oz) **white chocolate**

100 g (3½ oz) **unsalted butter**

3 **eggs**

1 **egg yolk**

100 g (3½ oz) **caster sugar**

2 tablespoons **double cream**

Roll out the pastry on a lightly floured surface until large enough to line a greased 24 cm (9½ inch) fluted, loose-bottomed flan tin (see page 11). Drape into the tin using a rolling pin. Press in place and trim off the excess. Prick with a fork, then chill for 15 minutes. Line with nonstick baking paper, add macaroni or beans and bake blind (see page 12) in a preheated oven, 190°C (375°F), Gas Mark 5, for 15 minutes. Remove the paper and macaroni or beans and bake for 5 minutes.

Melt the dark and white chocolate in separate bowls over simmering water (see page 11). Add three-quarters of the butter to the dark chocolate and the rest to the white chocolate. Leave until melted.

Whisk the eggs, egg yolk and sugar in a third bowl for 3–4 minutes until doubled in volume (but not so thick as to leave a trail). Fold two-thirds into the dark chocolate mixture, then pour into the cooked tart case. Fold the cream into the white chocolate to loosen it, then fold in the remaining whisked egg mixture. Spoon over the dark chocolate layer to completely cover.

Reduce the oven to 160°C (325°F), Gas Mark 3, and cook the tart for 20 minutes until just set with a slight wobble to the centre. Cool for at least 1 hour. Pipe double lines of melted dark chocolate and leave for at least 30 minutes before serving.

For dark chocolate tart, melt 300 g (10 oz) plain dark chocolate with 100 g (3½ oz) butter. Whisk the eggs and sugar as above and fold into the chocolate mixture. Pour into the baked tart case and cook for 15 minutes. Dust with sifted cocoa to serve.

mini nectarine & blueberry tarts

Makes **12**
Preparation time **15 minutes**
Cooking time **6–8 minutes**

25 g (1 oz) **unsalted butter**
2 teaspoons **olive oil**
4 sheets chilled **filo pastry**,
    each 30 x 18 cm (12 x
    7 inches) or 65 g (2½ oz)
    total weight
a little **flour**, for dusting
2 tablespoons **red berry jam**
juice of ½ **orange**
4 ripe **nectarines**, halved,
    pitted and sliced
150 g (5 oz) **blueberries**
icing sugar, for dusting

Heat the butter and oil in a small saucepan until the butter has melted.

Unfold the pastry on a lightly floured surface and separate into sheets. Brush lightly with the butter mixture, then cut into 24 pieces, each 10 x 8 cm (4 x 3½ inches).

Arrange a piece in each of the sections of a deep 12-hole muffin tin, then add a second piece at a slight angle to the first pieces to give a pretty jagged edge to each pastry case.

Bake in a preheated oven, 180°C (350°F), Gas Mark 4, for 6–8 minutes until golden. Meanwhile, warm the jam and orange juice in a saucepan, then add the nectarines and blueberries and warm through.

Lift the tart cases carefully out of the muffin tin and transfer to a serving dish. Fill the cases with the warm fruits and dust with sifted icing sugar. Serve with cream or ice cream.

For honeyed grape tarts, make up the tart cases as above. In a saucepan, cook 300 g (10 oz) halved ruby seedless grapes, 175 ml (6 fl oz) red grape juice and 1 tablespoon honey for 5 minutes. Lift out the grapes with a draining spoon, then boil the juice until syrupy. Return the grapes to the pan, then leave to cool. Mix 250 g (8 oz) Greek yogurt with 2 tablespoons runny honey, spoon into the tart cases and top with the cooled syrupy grapes.

white chocolate & raspberry puffs

Serves **6**
Preparation time **20 minutes**,
 plus chilling
Cooking time **15 minutes**

375 g (12 oz) chilled **ready-
 made puff pastry** or
 homemade flaky pastry
 (see page 15)
a little **flour**, for dusting
200 ml (7 fl oz) **double cream**
½ **vanilla pod**
200 g (7 oz) **white chocolate**,
 chopped
150 g (5 oz) **raspberries**
icing sugar, for dusting

Roll out the pastry dough on a lightly floured surface until it is a rectangle 2.5 mm (⅛ inch) thick. Cut it into 6 rectangles, each 12 x 7 cm (5 x 3 inches), and put them on a baking sheet. Chill for 30 minutes. Bake in a preheated oven, 200°C (400°F), Gas Mark 6, for 15 minutes until the pastry is puffed and golden. Transfer to a wire rack to cool.

Put the cream and vanilla pod in a saucepan and heat gently until it reaches boiling point. Remove from the heat and scrape the seeds from the vanilla pod into the cream (discard the pod). Immediately stir in the chocolate and continue stirring until it has melted. Cool, chill for 1 hour until firm, then whisk until spreadable.

Split the pastries in half crossways and fill each with white chocolate cream and raspberries. Serve dusted with sifted icing sugar.

For strawberry custard creams, make the pastry rectangles as above, then cool. Whip 150 ml (¼ pint) double cream until it forms soft swirls, then fold in a 125 g (4 oz) tub of ready-made custard. Split and fill the pastries with custard cream and 250 g (8 oz) sliced strawberries. Dust the tops with sifted icing sugar before serving.

banoffee pie

Serves **6**
Preparation time **35 minutes**,
    plus chilling and cooling
Cooking time **8 minutes**

200 g (7 oz) **unsalted butter**
2 tablespoons **golden syrup**
250 g (8 oz) **digestive
    biscuits**, crushed
100 g (3½ oz) **dark
    muscovado sugar**
400 g (13 oz) can **full-fat
    condensed milk**
300 ml (½ pint) **double cream**
3 small **bananas**
juice of 1 **lemon**
plain dark chocolate, grated,
    to decorate

Melt half the butter and the syrup in a saucepan, add the biscuit crumbs and mix well. Tip into a greased 20 cm (8 inch) springform tin and press evenly over the base and up the sides almost to the tin's top. Chill.

Heat the remaining butter and the sugar in a nonstick frying pan until the butter has melted and the sugar dissolved. Add the condensed milk and cook over a medium heat, stirring continuously, for 4–5 minutes until the mixture thickens and it begins to smell of caramel (don't have the heat too high or the condensed milk will burn).

Take the pan off the heat and leave the mixture to cool for 1–2 minutes, then pour into the biscuit case. Allow to cool completely, then chill for at least 1 hour.

Whip the cream until it forms soft peaks just before serving. Halve the bananas lengthways, then slice them and toss them in the lemon juice. Fold two-thirds into the cream, then spoon over the toffee layer. Arrange the remaining bananas on top. Loosen the edge of the biscuit crust with a palette knife, then remove the tin and transfer the pie to a serving plate. Sprinkle with grated chocolate and serve cut into wedges.

For banoffee ice cream sundae, make the toffee sauce as above but cook for just 2 minutes so that it is runnier, then leave to cool. Layer the sliced bananas in 6 glasses with 12 scoops vanilla ice cream, 6 crumbled brandy snap biscuits and a drizzle of the sauce, reheated if very thick. Sprinkle the top with chocolate curls or grated chocolate.

papaya, lime & mango tartlets

Makes **20**
Preparation time **35 minutes**
Cooking time **15–20 minutes**

250 g (8 oz) chilled **ready-made** or **homemade sweet shortcrust pastry** (see page 15)
a little **flour**, for dusting
thinly grated rind and juice of 2 large, juicy **limes**
6 tablespoons **double cream**
150 ml (¼ pint) **full-fat condensed milk**
2 tablespoons finely diced **papaya**
2 tablespoons finely diced **mango**
lime rind, to decorate

Roll out the pastry on a lightly floured surface to a 2.5 mm (⅛ inch) thickness, then, using a 5 cm (2 inch) round biscuit or pastry cutter, stamp out 20 rounds. Use the pastry rounds to line 20 x 5 cm (2 inch) mini tartlet tins (see page 11). Prick the pastry bases with a fork. Line with nonstick baking paper, add macaroni or beans and bake blind (see page 12) in a preheated oven, 190°C (375°F), Gas Mark 5, for 10 minutes, then remove the paper and macaroni or beans and return the cases to the oven for 5–10 minutes or until they are crisp and golden. Remove from the oven.

Put the lime rind in a blender with the cream and condensed milk and pulse until well combined. With the motor running, slowly pour in the lime juice and process until blended. (Alternatively, mix well by hand.) Transfer to a bowl, cover and chill in the refrigerator for 3–4 hours or until firm.

Put the cases on a serving platter and spoon the lime mixture into each case. Mix the mango with the papaya and, using a teaspoon, top the cases. Decorate with lime rind and serve immediately.

For summer berry tartlets, make the pastry cases and filling as above. Spoon the filling into the cases. Warm 3 tablespoons redcurrant jelly with the grated rind and juice of 1 lime, cook until syrupy, then stir in 150 g (5 oz) blueberries and 150 g (5 oz) raspberries. Spoon over the top of the tartlets.

deliciously
decadent

strawberry rosé jelly & syllabub

Serves **6**

Preparation time **25 minutes**, plus soaking and chilling

4 tablespoons **water**
1 sachet or 3 teaspoons **powdered gelatine**
40 g (1½ oz) **caster sugar**
500 ml (17 fl oz) **rosé wine**
250 g (8 oz) small **strawberries**, hulled and halved

Syllabub cream
finely grated rind of 1 **lemon**
25 g (1 oz) **caster sugar**
6 tablespoons **rosé wine**
250 ml (8 fl oz) **double cream**

Spoon the measured water into a small heatproof bowl or mug, then sprinkle the gelatine over the top, tilting the bowl so that the dry powder is completely absorbed by the water. Leave to soak for 5 minutes.

Heat the bowl or mug in a small pan of simmering water for 5 minutes or until a clear liquid forms. Take off the heat, then stir in the sugar until dissolved. Cool slightly, then gradually mix into the rosé wine.

Divide the strawberries between 6 tall Champagne-style glasses. Pour the rosé jelly mixture over and chill in the refrigerator until the jelly is set.

Mix the lemon rind, sugar and wine for the syllabub together and set aside. When ready to serve, whip the cream until it forms soft swirls, then gradually whisk in the lemon rind mixture. Spoon over the jellies.

For buck's fizz jellies, dissolve the gelatine as above, add 25 g (1 oz) caster sugar and when cool mix in 200 ml (7 fl oz) blood (or ordinary) orange juice and 500 ml (17 fl oz) cheap dry sparkling white wine. Divide 150 g (5 oz) fresh or frozen raspberries between the glasses, then top up with the jelly. Chill until set and serve plain.

chilled blackcurrant & mint soufflé

Serves **6**
Preparation time **40 minutes**,
  plus chilling
Cooking time **18–20 minutes**

250 g (8 oz) **blackcurrants**,
  defrosted if frozen
6 tablespoons **water**
4 teaspoons **powdered
  gelatine**
4 **eggs**, separated
200 g (7 oz) **caster sugar**
250 ml (8 fl oz) **double cream**
5 tablespoons finely chopped
  fresh mint
icing sugar, for dusting

Wrap a double thickness strip of nonstick baking paper around a 13 cm (5½ inch) diameter x 6 cm (2½ inch) deep soufflé dish so the paper stands 6 cm (2½ inches) above the dish top. Put the blackcurrants and 2 tablespoons of the water in a saucepan, cover and cook gently for 5 minutes until softened. Blend until smooth, then press through a sieve.

Put the remaining water in a small heatproof bowl and sprinkle over the gelatine, making sure the water absorbs all the powder. Set aside for 5 minutes, then stand the bowl in a pan half-filled with boiling water and simmer for 3–4 minutes, stirring occasionally, until the gelatine dissolves to a clear liquid.

Put the yolks and sugar in a large heatproof bowl and place over a pan of simmering water so the bowl's base is not touching the water. Whisk for 10 minutes or until the eggs are very thick and pale, and leave a trail when lifted above the mixture. Remove from the heat and continue whisking until cool. Fold in the dissolved gelatine in a thin, steady stream, then fold in the purée.

Whip the cream softly, then fold into the soufflé mix with the mint. Whisk the whites into stiff, moist-looking peaks. Fold a large spoonful into the soufflé mixture to loosen it, then gently fold in the remaining whites. Pour the mixture into the soufflé dish so that it stands above the rim of the dish. Chill for 4 hours or until set.

Remove the string and paper. Arrange 4–5 strips of nonstick baking paper over the soufflé top so some overlap, then dust with sifted icing sugar. Lift off the strips and serve immediately or the sugar will dissolve.

summer berry sponge

Serves **6–8**
Preparation time **30 minutes**,
  plus cooling
Cooking time **10–12 minutes**

4 eggs
100 g (3½ oz) **caster sugar**
100 g (3½ oz) **plain flour**
finely grated rind and
  2 tablespoons juice of
  1 lemon
150 ml (¼ pint) **double cream**
150 g (5 oz) **fromage frais**
3 tablespoons **lemon curd**
500 g (1 lb) small
  strawberries, halved
150 g (5 oz) **blueberries**
4 tablespoons **redcurrant jelly**
1 tablespoon **water** (or **lemon
  juice**)

Whisk the eggs and caster sugar in a large bowl until very thick and the mixture leaves a trail when lifted. Sift the flour over the surface of the eggs, then fold in very gently. Add the lemon rind and juice and fold in until just mixed. Pour the mixture into a greased, floured 25 cm (10 inch) sponge flan tin, tilting the tin to ease into an even layer.

Bake in a preheated oven, 180°C (350°F), Gas Mark 4, for 10–12 minutes until the top of the sponge is golden and the centre springs back when lightly pressed. Cool the sponge in the tin for 5–10 minutes, then carefully turn it out on to a wire rack to cool.

Whip the cream until it forms soft swirls, then fold in the fromage frais and lemon curd. Transfer the sponge to a serving plate, spoon the cream into the centre, spread into an even layer, then top with the strawberries and blueberries. Warm the redcurrant jelly in a small saucepan with the measured water (or lemon juice), then brush over the fruit.

For strawberry sponge flan with Pimm's, make the sponge flan as above, then fill with 300 ml (½ pint) whipped cream flavoured with the grated rind of ½ orange. Top with 500 g (1 lb) sliced strawberries and 150 g (5 oz) raspberries that have been soaked in 3 tablespoons undiluted Pimm's and 2 tablespoons caster sugar for 30 minutes.

hazelnut meringue gateau

Serves **8–10**
Preparation time **30 minutes**,
   plus cooling and chilling
Cooking time **1–1¼ hours**

5 **eggs**, separated
300 g (10 oz) **caster sugar**
1 tablespoon **cornflour**
125 g (4 oz) **blanched
   hazelnuts**, toasted and
   finely ground
250 g (8 oz) **plain dark
   chocolate**, broken into
   pieces
200 ml (7 fl oz) **double cream**
cocoa powder, for dusting

Chocolate hazelnuts
50 g (2 oz) **plain dark
   chocolate**, broken into
   pieces
50 g (2 oz) **hazelnuts**

Line 3 baking sheets and draw a 23 cm (9 inch) circle
on each piece of baking paper.

Whisk the egg whites until stiff, then gradually whisk
in the sugar until thick and glossy (see page 10).
Fold in the cornflour and ground hazelnuts until evenly
incorporated and transfer the mixture to a large piping
bag fitted with a 1 cm (½ inch) plain nozzle. Starting in
the centre of each prepared circle, pipe the mixture in
a continuous coil, finishing just within the marked line.

Bake in a preheated oven, 150°C (300°F), Gas Mark
2, for 1–1¼ hours until lightly golden and dried out.
Remove from the oven and transfer to a wire rack to
cool completely. Peel away the baking paper.

Melt the chocolate (see page 11) together with the
cream over a pan of gently simmering water to make
the filling. Cool, then chill for 1 hour until thickened.

Melt the chocolate for the chocolate hazelnuts and use
a fork to dip in the hazelnuts until coated. Leave to set
on baking paper.

Beat the chocolate filling until it is light and fluffy
and use to sandwich the meringue layers together.
Decorate the gateau with the chocolate hazelnuts and
serve dusted with sifted cocoa powder.

For chocolate & almond gateau, replace the ground
hazelnuts with 125 g (4 oz) ground almonds and
fold into the egg whites and sugar with the cornflour.
Bake the meringue and fill as above. Coat 50 g (2 oz)
blanched almonds in melted chocolate and use as
above, finishing with a dusting of cocoa powder.

summer berry mousses

Serves **6**
Preparation time **45 minutes**,
  plus cooling and chilling
Cooking time **12–15 minutes**

3 eggs
75 g (3 oz) **caster sugar**
75 g (3 oz) **plain flour**, sifted

Mousse
2 teaspoons **powdered
  gelatine**
2 tablespoons **cold water**
2 **egg whites**
75 g (3 oz) **caster sugar**
150 ml (¼ pint) **double cream**
200 g (7 oz) **frozen summer
  fruits**, just defrosted, puréed

To decorate
a few whole **redcurrants** and
  raspberries and some
  strawberries, halved
a few small **fresh mint leaves**
icing sugar, for dusting

Whisk the eggs and sugar until they are very thick and the whisk leaves a trail when lifted. Gently fold in the flour. Line the base and sides of a tin with a base of 35 x 25 cm (14 x 10 inches). Pour in the mixture.

Bake in a preheated oven, 180°C (350°F), Gas Mark 4, for 12–15 minutes until the sponge is golden and springs back when pressed. Leave to cool in the tin.

Cut 12 x 7.5 cm (3 inch) circles from the sponge with a biscuit cutter. Cut 6 strips of plastic (a new plastic folder is ideal) measuring 27 x 7.5 cm (11 x 3 inches). Wrap a strip tightly around each of the sponge circles and secure with tape. Put on a baking sheet.

Sprinkle gelatine over the measured water in a bowl and leave to soak for 5 minutes. Stand the bowl in a pan of simmering water and leave until the gelatine has dissolved to a clear liquid. Whisk the egg whites until stiff peaks form, then gradually whisk in the sugar until thick and glossy (see page 10). Whip the cream in a second bowl. Trickle the gelatine into the cream and mix together, then fold in the fruit purée and meringue.

Divide the mixture between the plastic collars, then top with the remaining sponge circles. Chill the mousses for 4–5 hours until set. Remove the plastic, scatter each mousse with a few whole or halved berries, dust with sifted icing sugar and serve.

For peach melba mousses, make the mousses with 4 ripe peaches, puréed and sieved. Chill as above, then serve drizzled with 125 g (4 oz) puréed, sieved raspberries and a few extra whole raspberries.

baked ricotta cheesecake

Serves **6**
Preparation time **20 minutes**,
  plus cooling and chilling
Cooking time **47–50 minutes**

480 g (17 oz) **ricotta cheese**
425 g (15 oz) **cream cheese**
2 **eggs**
1 teaspoon **vanilla essence**
125 g (4 oz) **caster sugar**
½ small **orange**
1 teaspoon **whole cloves**
2 tablespoons **dark brown
  sugar**
1 **cinnamon stick**
175 ml (6 fl oz) **water**
375 g (12 oz) **red plums**,
  halved and pitted
2 tablespoons **redcurrant jelly**

Grease a 500 g (1 lb) loaf tin lightly and line the base and sides with nonstick baking paper. Blend the ricotta and cream cheese with the eggs, vanilla essence and caster sugar until smooth. Turn the mixture into the loaf tin and place in a small roasting tin. Pour hot water into the tin to a depth of 2.5 cm (1 inch) and bake in a preheated oven, 160°C (325°F), Gas Mark 3, for about 40 minutes or until lightly set. Lift the loaf tin out of the water and allow to cool in the tin.

Stud the orange with the cloves and place in a heavy-bottomed pan with the brown sugar, cinnamon and measured water. Bring the water to the boil, reduce the heat and add the plums. Cover and cook gently for 5 minutes or until just tender.

Lift out the plums and add the redcurrant jelly to the pan. Boil the liquid for about 2 minutes until reduced and syrupy. Remove the orange and cinnamon stick and pour the syrup over the plums. Let the syrup cool, then chill until ready to serve.

Remove the cheesecake from the tin, peel off the paper and cut into slices. Serve topped with the poached plums.

For baked ricotta cheesecake with tropical sauce, make the cheesecake as above, omitting the poached plums. Roughly chop the flesh of 1 large mango, then purée with the juice of 1 large orange and 1 lime. Sieve the purée, then mix with 1 tablespoon icing sugar and the seeds from 2 halved passion fruits. Serve with cheesecake slices.

lemon polenta cake

Serves **8–10**
Preparation time **20 minutes**, plus cooling
Cooking time **30 minutes**

125 g (4 oz) **plain flour**
1½ teaspoons **baking powder**
125 g (4 oz) **polenta**
3 **eggs**
2 **egg whites**
175 g (6 oz) **golden caster sugar**
grated rind and juice of 2 **lemons**
100 ml (3½ fl oz) **vegetable oil**
150 ml (¼ pint) **buttermilk**

Red wine strawberries
300 ml (½ pint) **red wine**
1 **vanilla pod**, split
150 g (5 oz) **caster sugar**
2 tablespoons **balsamic vinegar**
250 g (8 oz) **strawberries**, hulled

Sift the flour and baking powder into a bowl and stir in the polenta, then set aside. Whisk the eggs, egg whites and sugar together for 3–4 minutes until pale and thickened. Stir in the polenta mixture, lemon rind and juice, oil and buttermilk to form a smooth batter.

Pour the mixture into a greased and base-lined 25 cm (10 inch) springform cake tin. Bake in a preheated oven, 180°C (350°F), Gas Mark 4, for 30 minutes until risen and firm to the touch. Leave to cool in the tin for 10 minutes, then turn out on to a wire rack, remove lining paper and leave to cool.

Place the wine, vanilla pod and sugar in a saucepan and heat gently to dissolve the sugar. Increase the heat and simmer for 10–15 minutes until the mixture is reduced and syrupy. Leave to cool, then stir in the balsamic vinegar and strawberries.

Cut the lemon polenta cake into slices and serve with the red wine strawberries.

For polenta cake with lemon syrup, make up the cake as above. In a saucepan, heat the finely grated rind and juice of 2 lemons, 200 g (7 oz) caster sugar and 2 tablespoons of water, until the sugar has dissolved. Turn the hot cake out on to a serving plate, pour over the syrup and leave for 15 minutes to soak. Serve warm, in wedges, with cream or Greek yogurt.

coffee latte custards

Serves **6**
Preparation time **20 minutes**,
  plus chilling
Cooking time **30 minutes**

2 **eggs**
2 **egg yolks**
397 g (13¾ oz) can **full-fat
  condensed milk**
200 ml (7 fl oz) **strong black
  coffee**
150 ml (¼ pint) **double cream**
cocoa powder, for dusting
chocolate wafer biscuits,
  to serve

Whisk the eggs, egg yolks and condensed milk in a
bowl until just mixed. Gradually whisk in the coffee
until blended.

Strain the mixture, then pour into 6 small 125 ml
(4 fl oz) greased coffee cups. Transfer the cups to a
roasting tin. Pour hot water into the tin to come halfway
up the sides of the cups, then cook in a preheated
oven, 160°C (325°F), Gas Mark 3, for 30 minutes until
just set. Lift the cups out of the water, leave to cool,
then transfer to the refrigerator and chill for 4–5 hours.

Whip the cream until it forms soft swirls when ready to
serve. Spoon the cream over the top of the desserts,
dust with a little sifted cocoa powder and serve with
chocolate wafer biscuits.

For dark chocolate custards, bring 450 ml
(¾ pint) milk and 150 ml (¼ pint) double cream just
to the boil in a saucepan. Add 200 g (7 oz) plain dark
chocolate, broken into pieces, and leave to melt.
Mix 2 eggs and 2 egg yolks with 50 g (2 oz) caster
sugar and ¼ teaspoon ground cinnamon, then
gradually mix in the chocolate mixture and stir until
smooth. Strain into small dishes and bake as above.
Top with whipped cream and chocolate curls.

choc & chestnut roulade

Serves **8**

Preparation time **20 minutes**,
plus cooling

Cooking time **25 minutes**

125 g (4 oz) **plain dark
chocolate**, broken into
pieces

5 **eggs**, separated

175 g (6 oz) **caster sugar**,
plus extra to sprinkle

2 tablespoons **cocoa powder**,
sifted

250 g (8 oz) canned
**unsweetened chestnut
purée**

4 tablespoons **icing sugar**

1 tablespoon **brandy**

250 ml (8 fl oz) **double cream**

icing sugar, for dusting

Melt the chocolate (see page 11), then leave to cool for 5 minutes. Put the egg yolks in a bowl, add the sugar and whisk together for 5 minutes until pale and thickened. Stir in the melted chocolate and cocoa. Whisk the egg whites in a clean bowl until stiff and fold into the chocolate mixture until evenly combined.

Grease and line a 33 x 23 cm (13 x 9 inch) Swiss roll tin. Transfer the mixture to the tin, spreading it well into the corners, and smooth the surface with a palette knife. Bake in a preheated oven, 180°C (350°F), Gas Mark 4, for 20 minutes until risen and set.

Sprinkle a large sheet of baking paper with caster sugar. Remove the roulade from the oven and turn it out immediately on to the sugared paper. Carefully remove the lining paper and cover the roulade with a clean tea towel. Set aside to cool.

Put the chestnut purée and icing sugar in a food processor and purée until smooth (or combine well by hand). Transfer the mixture to a bowl and stir in the brandy. Gently whisk in the cream until light and fluffy. Spread the filling over the roulade, leaving a 1 cm (½ inch) border, and roll it up from one short end to form a log. Serve dusted with sifted icing sugar.

For Black Forest roulade, make and bake the roulade as above. Whip the double cream until it forms soft swirls, then whisk in 2 tablespoons icing sugar and 2 tablespoons kirsch, if liked. Spread over the roulade, then sprinkle with a 425 g (14 oz) can of pitted cherries, well drained. Roll up the roulade and dust with icing sugar.

amaretti & chocolate custard

Serves **4**
Preparation time **20 minutes**,
   plus chilling
Cooking time **55–65 minutes**

175 g (6 oz) **granulated
   sugar**
125 ml (4 fl oz) **cold water**
2 tablespoons **cocoa powder**
4 tablespoons **boiling water**
2 **eggs**
2 **egg yolks**
65 g (2½ oz) **amaretti
   biscuits**, finely crushed
450 ml (¾ pint) **milk**
150 ml (¼ pint) **strong black
   coffee**

To decorate
chocolate curls or a few
   amaretti biscuits, crumbled

Dissolve 125 g (4 oz) sugar in the water, occasionally stirring. When dissolved, increase the heat and boil for 5 minutes without stirring until golden brown, keeping a watchful eye towards the end of the cooking time.

Mix the cocoa in a small bowl with 2 tablespoons of the boiling water. Mix the remaining sugar with the eggs, egg yolks and biscuits in a second larger bowl.

Take the syrup off the heat as soon as it caramelizes. Add the remaining boiling water and tilt to mix. Pour into a 900 ml (1½ pint) ovenproof china dish. Tilt to coat the base and halfway up the sides. Stand in a roasting tin.

Pour the milk into the drained caramel pan and bring just to the boil. Stir the cocoa mix into the egg mixture, then gradually whisk in the hot milk, then the coffee. Slowly pour into the caramel-lined dish.

Fill the tin with hot water halfway up the sides of the dish, then cook in a preheated oven, 160°C (325°F), Gas Mark 3, for 50–60 minutes until the custard has just set but still wobbles slightly in the centre.

Take dish out of tin, leave to cool, then chill for 4–5 hours or overnight. To turn out, stand in just-boiled water for 10 seconds, then invert on a plate with a rim. Decorate with chocolate curls or crumbled biscuits.

For crème caramels, make the caramel as above. Mix 2 whole eggs and 2 egg yolks with 2 tablespoons sugar and ½ teaspoon vanilla essence. Warm 600 ml (1 pint) milk, whisk into the eggs, then divide among 4 x 250 ml (8 fl oz) metal moulds. Cook as above in a roasting tin of water for 30 minutes. Cool and chill.

hazelnut & pear roulade

Serves **6–8**

Preparation time **30 minutes**, plus cooling

Cooking time **18–20 minutes**

125 g (4 oz) **hazelnuts**

5 **eggs**, separated

175 g (6 oz) **caster sugar**, plus extra for sprinkling

1 just-ripe **pear**, peeled and coarsely grated

200 g (7 oz) **mascarpone cheese**

2 tablespoons **icing sugar**

250 g (8 oz) **fresh apricots**, roughly chopped

Grease and line a 30 x 23 cm (12 x 9 inch) roasting tin with nonstick baking paper, snipping diagonally into the corners so it lines the base and sides. Place the nuts on a piece of foil and toast under the grill for 3–4 minutes until golden. Roughly chop 2 tablespoons and reserve for decoration, then finely chop the remainder.

Whisk the yolks and sugar until they are thick and pale and the whisk leaves a trail. Fold in the finely chopped hazelnuts and pear. Whisk the whites into stiff, moist-looking peaks. Fold a large spoonful into the nut mix to loosen it, then gently fold in the remaining egg whites.

Spoon the mixture into the prepared tin. Bake the roulade in a preheated oven, 180°C (350°F), Gas Mark 4, for 15 minutes until golden brown and the top feels spongy. Cover and leave to cool for at least 1 hour.

Beat the mascarpone and icing sugar together until soft. On a work surface, cover a damp tea towel with baking paper and sprinkle with sugar. Turn the roulade on to the paper and remove the tin and lining paper.

Spread the roulade with the mascarpone mixture, then with the apricots. Roll up the roulade, starting from the short end nearest you, using the paper and tea towel to help. Transfer the roulade to a serving plate, sprinkle over the reserved hazelnuts and cut into thick slices.

For hazelnut, pear & chocolate roulade, make the roulade as above. Warm 150 g (5 oz) chocolate and hazelnut spread in the microwave for 20 seconds, then gently spread over the roulade. Whip 250 ml (8 fl oz) double cream, spoon over the top, then roll up.

gooseberry fool with lemon thins

Serves **6**
Preparation time **30 minutes**,
  plus cooling
Cooking time **20–25 minutes**

500 g (1 lb) **gooseberries**,
  topped and tailed
75 g (3 oz) **caster sugar**
2 tablespoons **concentrated
  elderflower cordial**
2 tablespoons **water**
150 ml (¼ pint) **double cream**
135 g (4½ oz) can or carton
  custard

Lemon thins
50 g (2 oz) **unsalted butter**
50 g (2 oz) **caster sugar**
50 g (2 oz) **golden syrup**
grated rind 1 **lemon**, plus
  1 tablespoon of the juice
125 g (4 oz) **plain flour**
½ teaspoon **bicarbonate
  of soda**
icing sugar, for dusting

Cook the gooseberries with the sugar, cordial and measured water in a covered saucepan for 10 minutes until soft. Purée the gooseberries and their cooking juices in a liquidizer or food processor until smooth, or rub through a sieve. Leave to cool.

Whip the cream until it forms soft swirls, then fold in the custard and gooseberry purée. Spoon into small glasses and chill.

Heat the butter, sugar, syrup and lemon rind and juice for the biscuits in a small saucepan until the butter has melted and sugar dissolved. Stir in the flour and bicarbonate of soda and mix until smooth.

Drop teaspoons of the mixture on to 2 greased baking sheets, well spaced apart, then bake in a preheated oven, 180°C (350°F), Gas Mark 4, for 10–12 minutes until browning around the edges. Cool for 10 minutes, then loosen and transfer to a wire rack. Dust with sifted icing sugar and serve with the fool.

For nectarine & orange fool, chop the flesh of 4 ripe nectarines, then cook them in a covered saucepan with the sugar and 4 tablespoons of fresh orange juice (no water or cordial) for 10 minutes until tender. Purée and finish as above. Add the grated rind of ½ orange and 1 tablespoon juice to the biscuits instead of the lemon.

strawberry & lavender soufflés

Serves **6**
Preparation time **40 minutes**,
plus chilling
Cooking time **13–14 minutes**

500 g (1 lb) **fresh
strawberries**, hulled
4 tablespoons **water**
4 teaspoons **powdered
gelatine**
4 **eggs**, separated
150 g (5 oz) **caster sugar**
4–5 **lavender sprigs**, petals
crumbled and stems
discarded
250 ml (8 fl oz) **double cream**
few drops **pink** or **red food
colouring** (optional)
small bunch **lavender**, to
decorate

Attach soufflé collars to 6 individual soufflé dishes,
7.5 cm (3 inches) in diameter, 4 cm (1½ inches) deep,
so that the paper rises 4 cm (1½ inches) above the top.
Slice 6 strawberries and divide them among the dishes.
Blend the remaining strawberries to a coarse purée.

Pour the measured water into a small heatproof bowl
and sprinkle over the gelatine. Set aside for 5 minutes,
then stand the bowl in a pan half-filled with boiling
water and simmer for 3–4 minutes, stirring occasionally,
until the gelatine dissolves to a clear liquid.

Put the egg yolks, sugar and lavender petals in a large
heatproof bowl and stand over a pan of simmering
water so the base does not touch the water. Whisk with
a hand-held electric whisk (or rotary hand or balloon
whisk) for 10 minutes or until the eggs are very thick
and pale and the whisk leaves a trail. Remove the bowl
from the heat and continue whisking until cool.

Gradually fold in the dissolved gelatine in a thin,
steady stream, then fold in the strawberry purée.

Softly whip the cream, then fold into the soufflé
mixture with the food colouring, if using. Chill if the
mixture is very soft.

Whisk the egg whites into stiff, moist-looking peaks.
Fold a large spoonful into the soufflé mixture to loosen
it, then gently fold in the remaining egg whites. Pour
the mixture into the prepared soufflé dishes so that it
stands above the rim. Chill for 4 hours or until set.

Peel back the paper collars and tuck a few trimmed
lavender stems under the string to serve.

pavlovas with orange cream

Serves **6**
Preparation time **25 minutes**,
  plus cooling
Cooking time **1¼–1½ hours**

100 g (3½ oz) **plain dark
  chocolate**, broken into
  pieces, plus a little extra,
  grated, to decorate
3 **egg whites**
175 g (6 oz) **caster sugar**
1 teaspoon **cornflour**
1 teaspoon **white wine
  vinegar**
½ teaspoon **vanilla essence**
250 ml (8 fl oz) **double cream**
2 **oranges**

Melt the chocolate (see page 11), then leave to cool for 10 minutes. Whisk the egg whites in a large bowl until stiff, moist-looking peaks form. Gradually whisk in the sugar and continue to whisk until the meringue is thick and glossy (see page 10).

Mix the cornflour with the vinegar and vanilla essence, then fold into the meringue. Add the melted chocolate and fold together briefly for a marbled effect. Spoon the meringue into 6 mounds on a large baking sheet lined with nonstick baking paper, then swirl into circles with the back of the spoon, making a slight indentation in the centre.

Bake in a preheated oven, 110°C (225°F), Gas Mark ½, for 1¼–1½ hours or until the pavlovas may be easily lifted off the paper. Leave to cool.

Whip the cream, when ready to serve, until it forms soft swirls. Grate the rind of 1 orange and fold into the cream. Slice off the top and bottom of each orange, then cut away the rest of the peel. Remove the segments, add any juice to the cream, then spoon this over the pavlovas. Arrange the segments and grate a little dark chocolate on top.

For strawberry & lychee pavlovas, make the meringue as above, omitting the chocolate, and bake for just 50–60 minutes. Fill with 250 ml (8 fl oz) whipped double cream flavoured with the grated rind of 1 lime and 2 tablespoons icing sugar. Top with a 425 g (14 oz) can pitted lychees, drained and quartered, and 250 g (8 oz) sliced strawberries.

vanilla crème brûlée

Serves **6**
Preparation time **20 minutes**,
  plus standing and chilling
Cooking time **25–30 minutes**

1 **vanilla pod**
600 ml (1 pint) **double cream**
8 **egg yolks**
65 g (2½ oz) **caster sugar**
3 tablespoons **icing sugar**

Slit the vanilla pod lengthways and place it in a saucepan. Pour the cream into the pan, then bring almost to the boil. Take off the heat and allow to stand for 15 minutes. Lift the pod out of the cream and, holding it against the side of the saucepan, scrape the black seeds into the cream. Discard the rest of the pod.

Use a fork to mix together the egg yolks and caster sugar in a bowl. Reheat the cream, then gradually mix it into the eggs and sugar. Strain the mixture back into the saucepan.

Place 6 ovenproof ramekins in a roasting tin, then divide the custard between them. Pour warm water around the dishes to come halfway up the sides, then bake in a preheated oven, 180°C (350°F), Gas Mark 4, for 20–25 minutes until the custard is just set with a slight softness at the centre.

Leave the dishes to cool in the water, then lift them out and chill in the refrigerator for 3–4 hours. About 25 minutes before serving, sprinkle with the icing sugar and caramelize using a blowtorch (or under a hot grill), then leave at room temperature.

For Amaretto brûlée, omit the vanilla pod. Mix the egg yolks and sugar as above, bring the cream almost to the boil, then immediately mix into the egg yolks adding 125 ml (4 fl oz) Amaretto di Saronno liqueur. Strain and continue as above. When chilled, sprinkle with 6 teaspoons flaked almonds, then the sugar, and caramelize as above.

blueberry & cherry cheesecake

Serves **6**
Preparation time **30 minutes**,
  plus chilling
Cooking time **5 minutes**

75 g (3 oz) **unsalted butter**
2 tablespoons **golden syrup**
175 g (6 oz) **digestive
  biscuits**, crushed
300 g (10 oz) tub **full-fat soft
  cheese**
200 g (7 oz) **fat-free fromage
  frais**
50 g (2 oz) **caster sugar**
grated rind and juice of
  1 **lemon**
½ teaspoon **vanilla essence**
150 ml (¼ pint) **double cream**

Topping
150 g (5 oz) **frozen
  blueberries**
150 g (5 oz) **frozen pitted
  cherries**
4 tablespoons **water**
2 tablespoons **caster sugar**
2 teaspoons **cornflour**

Melt the butter in a saucepan with the golden syrup, then stir in the biscuit crumbs and mix well. Tip the mixture into a greased 20 cm (8 inch) springform tin and press over the base and two-thirds of the way up the sides with the back of a spoon. Chill.

Scoop the soft cheese into a mixing bowl and break down with a spoon. Stir in the fromage frais, sugar, lemon rind and vanilla essence, then gradually mix in the lemon juice until smooth.

Whisk the cream in a second bowl until it forms soft swirls, then fold into the cheese mixture. Pour into the biscuit-lined tin and spread the surface level. Chill for 4–5 hours or overnight until firm.

Warm the frozen fruits in a pan with the measured water and sugar for 3–4 minutes until defrosted. Blend the cornflour with a little extra water, add to the pan, bring to the boil, stirring, and cook for 1 minute until the sauce has thickened. Leave to cool.

Loosen the edge of the biscuit case when ready to serve, unclip the tin sides, lift off the base and transfer the cheesecake to a serving plate. Cut into wedges and serve with the fruit compôte drizzled over the top.

For lime, kiwifruit & grape cheesecake, add the grated rind and juice of 2 limes to the cheesecake mixture instead of the lemon. Spoon into the tin as above, then arrange 2 sliced kiwifruits and 150 g (5 oz) halved green and red seedless grapes in rings over the top while the filling is still soft. Chill until set, then remove from the tin and cut into wedges to serve.

raspberry & champagne brûlée

Serves **6**
Preparation time **20 minutes**,
  plus cooling
Cooking time **25 minutes**

250 g (8 oz) **fresh
  raspberries**, plus a few
  extra, dusted with icing
  sugar, to decorate (optional)
6 **egg yolks**
150 g (5 oz) **caster sugar**
125 ml (4 fl oz) **dry
  Champagne**
125 ml (4 fl oz) **double cream**
3 tablespoons **icing sugar**

Divide the raspberries among 6 ramekin dishes. Put the egg yolks and sugar in a large bowl and set it over a saucepan of simmering water, making sure the water does not touch the bottom of the bowl. Whisk the egg yolks and sugar until light and foamy, then gradually whisk in the Champagne, then the cream. Continue whisking for about 20 minutes until the custard is very thick and bubbly.

Pour the custard over the raspberries and leave to cool at room temperature for about 1 hour. Sprinkle the tops with the sifted icing sugar and caramelize with a blowtorch (or under a hot grill). Serve within 20–30 minutes, decorated with a few extra raspberries lightly dusted with icing sugar.

For cidered peach brûlée, divide the diced flesh of 2 ripe peaches among 6 ramekins. Whisk the egg yolks and sugar as above, then gradually whisk in 125 ml (4 fl oz) medium cider instead of the Champagne. Continue as above.

gingered pineapple trifle

Serves **4–5**
Preparation time **20 minutes**

200 g (7 oz) **Jamaican gingercake**, diced
½ **fresh pineapple**, sliced, cored, peeled and diced
grated rind and segmented flesh of 1 **orange**
2 **kiwifruits**, peeled, halved and sliced
3 tablespoons **rum**
425 g (14 oz) can or carton **custard**
300 ml (½ pint) **double cream**
grated rind of 1 **lime**

Arrange the gingercake in an even layer in the base of a 1.2 litre (2 pint) glass serving dish. Spoon the pineapple, orange segments and kiwifruits on top and drizzle with the rum. Pour the custard over the fruit and spread into an even layer.

Whip the cream in a bowl until it forms soft swirls, then fold in half the orange rind and half the lime rind. Spoon the cream over the custard, then sprinkle with the remaining fruit rinds. Chill until ready to serve.

For raspberry & peach trifle, dice 4 trifle sponges and sprinkle in the base of a glass dish instead of the gingercake. Add 150 g (5 oz) fresh raspberries and the diced flesh of 2 ripe peaches. Drizzle with 3 tablespoons dry sherry, then cover with custard as above. Whip the cream and flavour with the grated rind of 1 lemon, spoon it over the custard and sprinkle with 2 tablespoons toasted flaked almonds.

florentine vanilla cheesecake

Serves **8–10**
Preparation time **25 minutes**,
  plus chilling
Cooking time **45 minutes**

125 g (4 oz) **plain dark chocolate**
50 g (2 oz) **slivered almonds**, lightly toasted
2½ tablespoons **glacé citrus rind**, finely chopped
6 **glacé cherries**, finely chopped
175 g (6 oz) **digestive biscuits**, crushed
65 g (2½ oz) **unsalted butter**, melted
480 g (17 oz) **cream cheese**
1 teaspoon **vanilla essence**
150 ml (¼ pint) **double cream**
150 g (5 oz) **Greek yogurt**
125 g (4 oz) **caster sugar**
3 **eggs**

Grease a 20 cm (8 inch) loose-bottomed cake tin and line the sides with a strip of nonstick baking paper. Chop half the chocolate into small pieces. Lightly crush the almonds and mix them in a bowl with the chocolate, glacé fruit, biscuit crumbs and butter. Stir the mixture until well combined, then turn into the tin, packing it into the bottom and slightly up the sides to form a shell.

Beat the cream cheese and vanilla essence in a bowl until smooth. Beat in the cream, yogurt, sugar and eggs to make a smooth batter.

Pour the egg mixture over the biscuit base and bake in a preheated oven, 160°C (325°F), Gas Mark 3, for 45 minutes or until the surface feels just firm around the edges but is still wobbly in the centre. Turn off the heat and let the cheesecake cool in the oven. Transfer to the fridge and chill well.

Transfer to a serving plate and peel away the lining paper. Melt the remaining chocolate (see page 11) and drizzle it around the top edges of the cheesecake. Chill until ready to serve.

For American cherry cheesecake, make a plain biscuit case by heating 75 g (3 oz) butter together with 2 tablespoons golden syrup in a pan until the butter has melted. Stir in 175 g (6 oz) crushed digestive biscuits and use to line the tin as above. Make the filling and bake as above. Serve topped with a 425 g (14 oz) can of cherry pie filling.

rosemary panna cottas

Serves **6**
Preparation time **15 minutes**,
    plus soaking and chilling
Cooking time **15 minutes**

3 tablespoons **cold water**
1 sachet or 3 teaspoons
    powdered gelatine
450 ml (¾ pint) **double cream**
150 ml (¼ pint) **milk**
4 tablespoons **thick honey**
2 teaspoons very finely
    chopped **rosemary leaves**

Apricot compôte
200 g (7 oz) ready-to-eat
    dried apricots, sliced
300 ml (½ pint) **water**
1 tablespoon **thick-set honey**
2 teaspoons very finely
    chopped **rosemary leaves**

To decorate
small **rosemary sprigs**
caster sugar, for dusting

Spoon the measured water into a small heatproof bowl or mug. Sprinkle the gelatine over and tilt the bowl or mug so that all the dry powder is absorbed by the water. Leave to soak for 5 minutes.

Pour the cream and milk into a saucepan, add the honey and bring to the boil. Add the soaked gelatine, take the pan off the heat and stir until completely dissolved. Add the rosemary and leave for 20 minutes for the flavours to infuse, stirring from time to time. Pour the cream mixture into 6 individual 150 ml (¼ pint) metal moulds, straining if preferred. Leave to cool completely, then chill for 4–5 hours until set.

Put all the compôte ingredients into a saucepan, cover and simmer for 10 minutes, then leave to cool.

Dip the moulds into hot water for 10 seconds, loosen the edges, then turn out the panna cottas on to small serving plates and spoon the compôte around them. Lightly dust the rosemary sprigs with caster sugar and use to decorate the panna cottas.

For vanilla panna cottas, make the panna cotta as above but without the rosemary, adding the seeds from 1 slit vanilla pod and the pod itself as the cream mixture cools. Discard the pod just before pouring the mixture into the moulds, then continue as above. Turn out and serve with fresh raspberries.

pink grapefruit cream

Serves **4**
Preparation time **15 minutes**

2 pink **grapefruits**
5 tablespoons **dark brown**
  sugar, plus extra for
  sprinkling
250 ml (8 fl oz) **double cream**
150 g (5 oz) **Greek yogurt**
3 tablespoons **concentrated**
  elderflower cordial
½ teaspoon **ground ginger**
½ teaspoon **ground cinnamon**
brandy snaps, to serve
  (optional)

Grate the rind of 1 grapefruit finely, making sure you don't take any of the bitter white pith. Cut the skin and the white membrane off both grapefruits, and cut between the membranes to remove the segments. Place in a large dish, sprinkle with 2 tablespoons of the sugar and set aside.

Whisk the cream in a large bowl until thick but not stiff. Fold in the yogurt, elderflower cordial, spices, grapefruit rind and remaining sugar until smooth.

Spoon the mixture into attractive glasses, arranging the grapefruit segments between layers of grapefruit cream. Sprinkle the top with a little extra sugar, add the brandy snaps, if desired, and serve immediately.

For spiced orange cream, finely grate the rind of 2 large oranges, then cut away the pith and membrane to release the orange segments. Sprinkle with 2 tablespoons of the sugar and set aside. Whip the cream, then flavour as above, adding the orange rind in place of the grapefruit rind.

tuile baskets & strawberry cream

Serves **6**
Preparation time **40 minutes**
Cooking time **15–18 minutes**

2 **egg whites**
100 g (3½ oz) **caster sugar**
50 g (2 oz) **unsalted butter**,
  melted
few drops **vanilla essence**
50 g (2 oz) **plain flour**

Strawberry cream
250 ml (8 fl oz) **double cream**
4 tablespoons **icing sugar**,
  plus extra for dusting
2 tablespoons chopped **fresh
  mint**, plus extra leaves to
  decorate
250 g (8 oz) **strawberries**,
  halved or sliced, depending
  on size

Put the egg whites in a bowl and break up with a fork.
Stir in the caster sugar, then the butter and vanilla
essence. Sift in the flour and mix until smooth.

Drop 1 heaped tablespoon of the mixture on to a
baking sheet lined with nonstick baking paper. Drop a
second spoonful well apart from the first, then spread
each into a thin circle about 13 cm (5 inches) in
diameter. Bake in a preheated oven, 190°C (375°F),
Gas Mark 5, for 5–6 minutes until just beginning to
brown around the edges.

Add 2 more spoonfuls to a second paper-lined baking
sheet and spread thinly. Remove the baked tuiles from
the oven and put the second tray in. Allow the cooked
tuiles to firm up for 5–10 seconds, then carefully lift
them off the paper one at a time and drape each over
an orange. Pinch the edges into pleats and leave to
harden for 2–3 minutes, then carefully ease off the
oranges. Repeat until 6 tuiles have been made.

Whip the cream lightly, then fold in half the sugar, the
mint and the strawberries, reserving 6 strawberry
halves for decoration. Spoon into the tuiles, then top
with the mint leaves and the strawberry halves. Dust
with sifted icing sugar.

For fruit salad baskets, make the tuiles as above and
fill with 200 g (7 oz) sliced strawberries, 150 g (5 oz)
halved seedless ruby grapes, 2 kiwifruits, peeled,
halved and sliced, and 2 small ripe peaches. Top with
Greek yogurt and a drizzle of honey.

peach & chocolate vacherin

Serves **6–8**
Preparation time **30 minutes**,
plus cooling
Cooking time **1½–1¾ hours**

4 **egg whites**
125 g (4 oz) **caster sugar**
100 g (3½ oz) **light muscovado sugar**
150 g (5 oz) **plain dark chocolate**, broken into pieces

Filling
150 ml (¼ pint) **double cream**
150 g (5 oz) **Greek yogurt**
2 tablespoons **caster sugar**
3 ripe **peaches**, pitted and sliced

Line 2 baking sheets with nonstick baking paper and draw an 18 cm (7 inch) circle on each.

Whisk the egg whites in a large bowl until stiff, moist-looking peaks form. Mix the sugars together, then whisk in the sugar, a teaspoonful at a time, and continue whisking for 1–2 minutes until very thick and glossy (see page 10).

Divide the mixture between the lined baking sheets and spread into circles of even thickness between the marked lines. Bake in a preheated oven, 110°C (225°F), Gas Mark ¼, for 1½–1¾ hours or until the meringues may be easily lifted off the paper. Leave to cool in the switched-off oven.

Melt the chocolate (see page 11), then spread over the underside of each meringue, leaving about one-third of the chocolate in the bowl for decoration. Leave the meringues to harden, chocolate-side up.

Whip the cream, when ready to serve, until it forms soft swirls, then fold in the yogurt and sugar. Put one of the meringue circles on a serving plate, chocolate-side up, spread with the cream, then arrange peach slices on top. Cover with the second meringue, chocolate-side down. Decorate the top with the remainder of the melted chocolate, drizzled randomly.

For chocolate & chestnut vacherin, make the meringues as above. Spread with chocolate and leave to harden. Whip 150 ml (¼ pint) double cream, fold in a 210 g (7½ oz) can of sweetened chestnut purée and 150 g (5 oz) fromage frais, then fill the meringues.

apricot meringue swirl

Serves **8**
Preparation time **35 minutes**,
  plus cooling
Cooking time **25 minutes**

4 **egg whites**
250 g (8 oz) **caster sugar**,
  plus extra for sprinkling
1 teaspoon **cornflour**
1 teaspoon **white wine
  vinegar**
200 g (7 oz) ready-to-eat
  dried apricots
300 ml (½ pint) **water**
150 ml (¼ pint) **double cream**
150 g (5 oz) **fromage frais**

Whisk the egg whites until stiff peaks form. Gradually whisk in the sugar, then whisk for a few minutes more until the mixture is thick and glossy (see page 10).

Mix the cornflour and vinegar together until smooth. Fold into the meringue mixture.

Spoon into a 33 x 23 cm (13 x 9 inch) Swiss roll tin lined with nonstick baking paper snipped diagonally into the corners and standing a little above the top of the sides. Spread level. Bake in a preheated oven, 190°C (375°F), Gas Mark 5, for 10 minutes until biscuit-coloured and well risen. Reduce the heat to 160°C (325°F), Gas Mark 3, for 5 minutes until just firm to the touch and the top is slightly cracked.

Cover a clean tea towel with nonstick baking paper and sprinkle with a little sugar. Turn the hot meringue out on to the paper, remove the tin and leave to cool for 1–2 hours. Meanwhile, simmer the apricots in the water for 10 minutes until tender. Cool, then purée until smooth.

Peel the lining paper off the meringue when ready to serve, then spread with the apricot purée. Whip the cream until it forms soft swirls, then fold in the fromage frais and spoon over the apricot purée.

Roll up the meringue to make a log shape, starting from a short side and using the paper to help. Transfer to a serving plate and cut into thick slices to serve.

For kiwifruit & passion fruit swirl, make the meringue as above. Fill with 300 ml (½ pint) whipped double cream, then sprinkle with 3 chopped kiwifruits and the seeds from 3 passion fruits.

chilled out

lime & passion fruit crunch tart

Serves **6–8**
Preparation time **30 minutes**,
  plus chilling and freezing

100 g (3½ oz) **unsalted butter**
2 tablespoons **golden syrup**
250 g (8 oz) **digestive
  biscuits**, crushed
300 ml (½ pint) **double cream**
grated rind and juice of
  3 **limes**
400 g (13 oz) can **full-fat
  condensed milk**

To decorate
3 **passion fruits**, halved
150 g (5 oz) **blueberries**

Heat the butter and golden syrup in a saucepan, stir
in the biscuit crumbs and mix well. Tip into a greased
23 cm (9 inch) springform tin, and press over the base
of the tin with the end of a rolling pin. Chill while
making the filling.

Whip the cream in a large bowl until it forms soft
swirls. Add the lime rind and condensed milk and
gently fold together, then gradually mix in the lime
juice. Pour over the biscuit base and freeze for 4 hours
or overnight.

Loosen the edge of the pudding from the tin with
a round-bladed knife, remove the sides, then slide
off the base on to a serving plate. Spoon the seeds
from the passion fruits over the top, then scatter with
the blueberries. Allow to soften for 30 minutes before
cutting into slices to serve.

For chocolate orange crunch tart, make the biscuit
base using chocolate digestive biscuits. Omit the
lime rind and juice from the cream mixture, adding
the grated rind and juice from 1 large orange instead.
Freeze until solid, then decorate with 50 g (2 oz) plain
dark chocolate, melted (see page 11) and drizzled
randomly over the top. Return the dessert to the
freezer until required.

pistachio & yogurt semifreddo

Serves **6**
Preparation time **40 minutes**,
   plus cooling and freezing
Cooking time **10–15 minutes**

4 **eggs**, separated
175 g (6 oz) **caster sugar**
grated rind of 1 **lemon**
1½ teaspoons **rose water**
   (optional)
200 g (7 oz) **Greek yogurt**
½ **fresh pineapple**, sliced,
   halved and cored

Pistachio brittle
150 g (5 oz) **granulated
   sugar**
6 tablespoons **water**
100 g (3½ oz) **pistachio nuts**,
   roughly chopped

Make the brittle. Heat the sugar and measured water in a frying pan until it dissolves, stirring gently from time to time. Add the nuts, then increase the heat and boil the syrup for 5 minutes, without stirring, until pale golden. Quickly tip the mixture on to a greased baking sheet and leave to cool. Break the brittle in half, then crush half in a plastic bag with a rolling pin.

Whisk the egg whites until very stiff, then gradually whisk in half the sugar until thick and glossy. Whisk the egg yolks in a second bowl with the remaining sugar until very thick and pale and the mixture leaves a trail. Fold in the lemon rind and rose water, if using, then the yogurt and crushed brittle, then the egg whites. Pour into a plastic box and freeze for 4–5 hours until semi-frozen and firm enough to scoop.

Cook the pineapple slices on a hot barbecue or preheated griddle pan for 6–8 minutes, turning once or twice until browned. Divide between the serving plates, top with spoonfuls of semifreddo and decorate with broken pieces of the remaining brittle.

For rocky road ice cream, make the brittle with almonds, hazelnuts and pecan nuts instead of pistachios. Whisk the egg whites, then the eggs and sugar, as for the semifreddo, then fold 135 g (4½ oz) ready-made custard and 150 ml (¼ pint) whipped double cream into the yolks with the crushed brittle. Fold in the egg whites as above, then freeze. Serve scooped into glasses with wafer biscuits.

166

cherry almond ice cream

Serves **6**
Preparation time **20 minutes**,
  plus cooling and freezing
Cooking time **20 minutes**

150 ml (¼ pint) **milk**
50 g (2 oz) **ground almonds**
1 **egg**
1 **egg yolk**
75 g (3 oz) **caster sugar**
2–3 drops **almond essence**
500 g (1 lb) **red cherries**,
  pitted, or **cherry compôte**
25 g (1 oz) **slivered almonds**
150 ml (¼ pint) **double cream**

Pour the milk into a small saucepan and stir in the ground almonds. Bring to the boil, then set aside.

Put the egg and the yolk into a heatproof bowl with the sugar and beat until pale and thick. Pour on the milk and almond mixture. Place the bowl over a pan of gently simmering water and stir until thick. Stir in the almond essence and leave to cool.

Purée the cherries in a food processor or blender (or use cherry compôte), then stir into the custard.

Toss the slivered almonds in a heavy pan over a low heat to toast them. Leave to cool.

Whip the cream until it forms soft peaks. Fold the whipped cream into the cherry mixture.

Transfer the mixture to a freezer container, cover and freeze until firm, beating twice at hourly intervals. Stir the slivered almonds into the mixture at the last beating. (If using an ice-cream machine, pour the cherry mixture into the machine, add the cream, churn and freeze. Once frozen, fold through the slivered almonds.) Serve the ice cream in individual glasses.

For strawberry & coconut ice cream, soak 50 g (2 oz) desiccated coconut in 150 ml (¼ pint) hot milk. Mix egg and egg yolk with sugar and make into custard as above, omitting the almond essence. When cold, fold in 500 g (1 lb) puréed strawberries and 150 ml (¼ pint) whipped double cream. Freeze as above. Serve with extra strawberries.

gingered apricot crush

Serves **6**
Preparation time **25 minutes**,
  plus cooling and freezing
Cooking time **10 minutes**

250 g (8 oz) ready-to-eat
  dried apricots
300 ml (½ pint) **water**
250 ml (8 fl oz) **double cream**
200 g (7 oz) **fat-free fromage
  frais**
40 g (1½ oz) **caster sugar**
75 g (3 oz) or about 4 pieces
  stem ginger from a jar,
  drained and roughly chopped,
  plus 2 tablespoons syrup
  from jar
40 g (1½ oz) **ready-made
  mini meringues**

Put the apricots and measured water in a saucepan, cover and simmer for 10 minutes. Purée the apricots and cooking liquid in a food processor or liquidizer until smooth, or rub through a sieve. Cool.

Whip the cream in a bowl until it forms soft swirls. Gently fold in the fromage frais, caster sugar, chopped ginger and ginger syrup. Crumble the meringues into pieces, then fold into the cream.

Line a 1 kg (2 lb) loaf tin with two pieces of clingfilm at right angles to each other so that the edges overhang the tin. Spoon in alternate spoonfuls of cream and apricot purée. Run the handle of a teaspoon through the mixture to marble together. Then fold the clingfilm over the top. Freeze for 6 hours or overnight until firm, or longer if preferred.

Unfold the top of the clingfilm and leave the dessert at room temperature for 15 minutes to soften slightly. Cover with a chopping board, invert the tin on to the board and remove the tin. Peel off the clingfilm. Cut into thick slices and serve.

For lemon & pineapple crush, flavour the cream mix with the grated rind of 2 lemons and a 220 g (7½ oz) can of pineapple, drained and finely chopped, instead of the ginger and ginger syrup. Add the meringues as above. Layer in the lined loaf tin with 4 tablespoons lemon curd and marble together. Freeze, then serve sliced with a drizzle of puréed strawberries.

chocolate ice cream

Serves **4**
Preparation time **20 minutes**,
  plus cooling and freezing
Cooking time **10 minutes**

300 ml (½ pint) **double cream**
2 tablespoons **milk**
50 g (2 oz) **icing sugar**, sifted
½ teaspoon **vanilla essence**
125 g (4 oz) good-quality
  plain dark chocolate,
  broken into pieces
2 tablespoons **single cream**

Chocolate sauce (optional)
150 ml (¼ pint) **water**
3 tablespoons **caster sugar**
150 g (5 oz) **plain dark
  chocolate**, broken into
  pieces

Put the double cream and milk in a bowl and whisk until just stiff. Stir in the icing sugar and vanilla essence. Pour the mixture into a shallow freezer container and freeze for 30 minutes or until the ice cream begins to set around the edges. (This ice cream cannot be made in an ice-cream machine.)

Melt the chocolate (see page 11), together with the single cream, over a pan of gently simmering water. Stir until smooth, then set aside to cool.

Remove the ice cream from the freezer and spoon into a bowl. Add the melted chocolate and quickly stir it through the ice cream with a fork. Return the ice cream to the freezer container, cover and freeze until set. Transfer the ice cream to the refrigerator 30 minutes before serving, to soften slightly.

Heat all the ingredients for the chocolate sauce, if making, gently in a saucepan, stirring until melted. Serve immediately with scoops of the ice cream.

For chocolate double mint ice cream, make the ice cream as above, adding 2 tablespoons chopped fresh mint and 20 g (¾ oz) crushed peppermint sweets to the whipped cream and milk. Freeze as above, then stir in the melted dark chocolate mix.

lychee & coconut sherbet

Serves **4–6**
Preparation time **30 minutes**,
  plus freezing
Cooking time **2–4 minutes**

425 g (14 oz) can **pitted
  lychees in light syrup**
50 g (2 oz) **caster sugar**
400 ml (14 fl oz) can **full-fat
  coconut milk**
grated rind and juice of 1 **lime**,
  plus extra pared **lime rind**,
  to decorate (optional)
chocolate cups (see below),
  to serve (optional)
3 **kiwifruits**, peeled and cut
  into wedges, to decorate

Drain the syrup from the can of lychees into a saucepan, add the sugar and heat gently until the sugar has dissolved. Boil for 2 minutes, then take off the heat and leave to cool.

Purée the lychees in a food processor or liquidizer until smooth, or rub through a sieve. Mix with the coconut milk, lime rind and juice. Stir in the sugar syrup when it is cool.

Pour into a shallow plastic container and freeze for 4 hours or until mushy. Beat with a fork or blend in a food processor or liquidizer until smooth. Pour back into the plastic container and freeze for 4 hours or overnight until solid. (Alternatively, freeze in an electric ice-cream machine for 20 minutes, then transfer to a plastic box and freeze until required.)

Allow to soften for 15 minutes at room temperature before serving, then scoop into dishes or chocolate cups (see below) and decorate with kiwifruit wedges and pared lime rind curls, if liked.

For chocolate cups, to serve the sherbet in, melt 150 g (5 oz) plain dark chocolate over a pan of simmering water (see page 11), then divide between 4 squares of nonstick baking paper and spread into rough-shaped circles about 15 cm (6 inches) in diameter. Drape the paper over upturned glass tumblers, with the chocolate uppermost, so that the paper falls in soft folds. Chill until set, then lift the paper and chocolate off the tumblers, turn over and carefully ease the paper away.

fresh melon sorbet

Serves **4–6**
Preparation time **15 minutes**,
  plus freezing

1 **cantaloupe melon**,
  weighing **1** kg (**2** lb)
50 g (2 oz) **icing sugar**
juice of **1 lime** or small **lemon**
1 **egg white**

Cut the melon in half and scoop out and discard the seeds. Scoop out the melon flesh with a spoon and discard the shells.

Place the flesh in a food processor or blender with the icing sugar and lime or lemon juice and process to a purée. (Alternatively, rub through a sieve.) Pour into a freezer container, cover and freeze for 2–3 hours. If using an ice-cream machine, purée then pour into the machine, churn and freeze until half-frozen.

Whisk the melon mixture to break up the ice crystals. Then whisk the egg white until stiff and whisk it into the half-frozen melon mixture. Return to the freezer until firm. Alternatively, add whisked egg white to the ice-cream machine and churn until very thick.

Transfer the sorbet to the fridge 20 minutes before serving to soften slightly or scoop straight from the ice-cream machine. Scoop the sorbet into glass dishes to serve. To make differently coloured sorbet, make up three batches of sorbet using a cantaloupe melon in one and honeydew and watermelon in the others.

For gingered melon sorbet, peel and finely grate a 2.5 cm (1 inch) piece of root ginger, then stir into the melon purée. Scoop into small glasses and drizzle each glass with 1 tablespoon ginger wine.

watermelon & tequila granita

Serves **6**
Preparation time **20 minutes**,
  plus infusing and freezing
Cooking time **2 minutes**

1 **vanilla pod**
150 g (5 oz) **caster sugar**
150 ml (¼ pint) **water**
2 kg (4 lb) **watermelon**
2 tablespoons **lemon juice**
4 tablespoons **tequila**

Use a small, sharp knife to score the vanilla pod lengthways through to the centre. Put it in a pan with the sugar and the measured water. Heat gently until the sugar has dissolved and let the syrup infuse for 20 minutes.

Slice the watermelon into wedges and cut away the skin. Blend the flesh in a food processor or blender until smooth, or rub through a sieve.

Remove the vanilla pod from the syrup, scrape out the seeds with the tip of a knife and return them to the syrup. Beat to disperse them. Discard the pod.

Strain the watermelon purée into a freezer container and stir in the vanilla syrup, lemon juice and tequila. Freeze for 3–4 hours until it is turning mushy. Mash with a fork and refreeze for 2–3 hours until it reaches the mushy stage again. Repeat the process once or twice more until the granita is evenly mushy. Freeze until required.

Fork through the granita to break up the ice and pile it into tall glasses. Serve with long spoons.

For blackberry and apple granita, heat 300 ml (½ pint) water with 25 g (1 oz) caster sugar until the sugar has dissolved. Add 4 large Gala apples that have been peeled, cored and diced and 150 g (5 oz) blackberries, then cover and simmer for 10 minutes. Cool, then purée and mix with 300 ml (½ pint) extra water. Freeze as above until flakes of ice begin to form.

mint granita

Serves **6**
Preparation time **20 minutes**,
  plus cooling and freezing
Cooking time **4 minutes**

200 g (7 oz) **caster sugar**
300 ml (½ pint) **water**, plus
  extra to top up
pared rind and juice of
  3 **lemons**
25 g (1 oz) **fresh mint**, plus
  a few sprigs to decorate
icing sugar, for dusting

Put the sugar and measured water into a saucepan, add the lemon rind and gently heat until the sugar has dissolved. Increase the heat and boil for 2 minutes.

Tear the tips off the mint stems and finely chop to give about 3 tablespoons, then reserve. Add the larger mint leaves and stems to the hot syrup and leave for 1 hour to cool and for the flavours to develop.

Strain the syrup into a jug, add the chopped mint and top up to 600 ml (1 pint) with extra cold water. Pour into a small roasting tin and freeze the mixture for 2–3 hours or until mushy.

Break up the ice crystals with a fork, then return to the freezer for 2–3 more hours, breaking up with a fork once or twice until the mixture is the consistency of crushed ice. Serve now, spooned into small glass tumblers, decorated with tiny sprigs of mint dusted with icing sugar, or leave in the freezer until required. If leaving in the freezer, allow to soften for 15 minutes before serving. If frozen overnight or longer, break up with a fork before serving.

For iced ruby grapefruit granita, make a plain sugar syrup as above, omitting the lemon rind. When cool, halve 4 ruby grapefruits, squeeze the juice and reserve 4 halved shells. Strain the juice into the syrup instead of the lemon juice, then freeze as above. Serve the dessert spooned into the reserved grapefruit shells.

lemon & honey ice

Serves **4–6**
Preparation time **20–25 minutes**, plus cooling and freezing
Cooking time **2 minutes**

4 large or 6 medium **lemons**
about 4 tablespoons **water**
2 tablespoons **clear honey**
65 g (2½ oz) **caster sugar**
1 **fresh bay leaf** or **lemon balm** sprig
450 g (14½ oz) **natural yogurt** or **fromage frais**
strips of **lemon rind**, to decorate

Slice off the top of each lemon. Carefully scoop out all the pulp and juice with a teaspoon. Discard any white pith, skin and pips, then purée the pulp and juice in a food processor or blender, or rub through a sieve. You will need 150 ml (¼ pint) – if there is less than this, top it up with water.

Put the measured water, honey, sugar and bay leaf or lemon balm into a saucepan. Stir over a low heat until the sugar has dissolved, then leave to cool. Blend the mixture with the lemon purée and the yogurt or fromage frais. Don't remove the herb at this stage.

Pour into a freezer tray or shallow dish and freeze until lightly frozen, then gently fork the mixture and remove the herb. Return the ice to the freezer until firm.

Transfer to the refrigerator about 20 minutes before serving. Serve decorated with strips of lemon rind.

For buttered oranges, to accompany the ice, peel 6 satsumas and, leaving them whole, place on a foil square. Cut 50 g (2 oz) unsalted butter into 6 pieces, add a piece to each orange with 1 teaspoon light muscovado sugar and a pinch of ground cinnamon. Wrap the foil to enclose the ingredients, then put on a baking sheet and cook in a preheated oven, 180°C (350°F), Gas Mark 4, for 10 minutes. Serve hot with scoops of ice.

coffee and hazelnut choc ices

Serves **6**
Preparation time **25 minutes**,
 plus freezing
Cooking time **5–10 minutes**

1 tablespoon **instant coffee**
2 tablespoons **boiling water**
4 **egg yolks**
50 g (2 oz) **caster sugar**
3 tablespoons **liquid glucose**
300 ml (½ pint) **double cream**
100 g (3½ oz) **plain dark
 chocolate**, broken into
 pieces
25 g (1 oz) **hazelnuts**,
 toasted, roughly chopped
4 tablespoons **Kahlua coffee
 liqueur** or **coffee cream
 liqueur**, to serve

Dissolve the coffee in the boiling water. Put the egg yolks, sugar and liquid glucose in a large bowl set over a saucepan of simmering water and whisk for 5–10 minutes until very thick and the mixture leaves a trail when the whisk is lifted. Take the bowl off the heat and stand in cold water, then whisk until cool. Whip the cream in a second bowl until it forms soft swirls. Fold into the whisked yolks with the dissolved coffee.

Line a 20 cm (8 inch) shallow square cake tin with clingfilm, covering the inside of the tin completely. Pour in the coffee mixture and freeze for 3 hours until firm.

Melt the chocolate (see page 11) over a pan of gently simmering water. Spoon on to a baking sheet lined with nonstick baking paper and spread into a thin even layer. Sprinkle with the hazelnuts and chill until firm.

Lift out the coffee ice using the clingfilm. Cut the ice into 3 even-sized strips, then cut each strip into 4 rectangles. Cut the chocolate into slightly larger pieces, then lift off the paper with a palette knife.

Layer 3 chocolate rectangles with 2 rectangles of coffee ice in between to make 6 stacks. Put one stack on each serving plate, then drizzle the liqueur around the plate. Serve at once.

For double chocolate ices, follow the recipe above but replace the coffee with 125 g (4 oz) melted plain dark chocolate. Spoon into ramekin dishes lined with clingfilm and freeze until firm. Serve the desserts on plates drizzled with chocolate sauce (see page 172), topped with a few chocolate curls (see page 11).

iced chocolate mousses

Serves **6**
Preparation time **30 minutes**,
  plus cooling and freezing
Cooking time **10 minutes**

250 g (8 oz) **plain dark
  chocolate**
15 g (½ oz) **unsalted butter**
2 tablespoons **liquid glucose**
3 tablespoons **fresh orange
  juice**
3 **eggs**, separated
200 ml (7 fl oz) **double cream**

Make chocolate curls by paring the underside of the block of chocolate with a swivel-bladed vegetable peeler. If the curls are very small, microwave the chocolate in 10-second bursts on full power (or place in a warm oven) until the chocolate is soft enough to shape. When you have enough curls to decorate 6 mousses, break the remainder into pieces – you should have 200 g (7 oz) – and melt (see page 11).

Stir the butter and glucose into the chocolate, then mix in the orange juice. Stir the egg yolks one by one into the mixture until smooth. Take off the heat and leave to cool.

Whisk the egg whites until softly peaking. Whip the cream until it forms soft swirls. Fold the cream, then the egg whites, into the chocolate mix. Pour the mixture into 6 coffee cups or ramekin dishes.

Freeze for 4 hours or overnight until firm. Decorate the tops with chocolate curls.

For chilled chocolate & coffee mousses, omit the chocolate curls and instead melt 200 g (7 oz) plain dark chocolate, then add 15 g (½ oz) butter (omit the liquid glucose), 3 tablespoons strong black coffee and 3 egg yolks. Fold in 3 whisked egg whites, then pour the mixture into 4 small dishes or glasses and chill in the refrigerator for 4 hours until set. Whip 125 ml (4 fl oz) double cream until it forms soft swirls, then fold in 2 tablespoons coffee cream liqueur, if liked. Spoon on to the top of the mousses and decorate with a little sifted cocoa powder.

honeyed banana ice cream

Serves **4–6**
Preparation time **15 minutes**,
  plus freezing and setting

500 g (1 lb) **bananas**
2 tablespoons **lemon juice**
3 tablespoons **thick honey**
150 g (5 oz) **natural yogurt**
100 g (3½ oz) **chopped nuts**
150 ml (¼ pint) **double cream**
2 **egg whites**

Praline
50 ml (2 fl oz) **water**
170 g (6 oz) **caster sugar**
2 tablespoons **golden syrup**
175 g (6 oz) **toasted
  almonds**

Put the bananas in a bowl with the lemon juice and mash until smooth. Stir in the honey, followed by the yogurt and nuts, and beat well. Place the banana mix and the cream in an ice-cream machine. Churn and freeze following the manufacturer's instructions until half frozen. Alternatively, whisk the cream until it forms soft swirls, then fold into the banana mix and freeze in a plastic container for 3–4 hours until partially frozen.

Whisk the egg whites lightly until they form soft peaks. Add to the ice-cream machine and continue to churn and freeze until completely frozen. Alternatively, break up the ice cream in the plastic container with a fork, then fold in the whisked egg white and freeze until firm.

Make the praline. Pour the measured water into a heavy saucepan and add the sugar and golden syrup. Simmer gently until the sugar has dissolved, then cook to a caramel-coloured syrup. Place the toasted almonds on a lightly greased piece of foil and pour the syrup over. Leave to set for 1 hour. Once set, break up into irregular pieces and serve with the ice cream.

For honeyed banana ice cream with sticky glazed bananas, make the ice cream as above. When ready to serve, heat 25 g (1 oz) unsalted butter in a frying pan, add 3 thickly sliced bananas and fry until just beginning to soften. Sprinkle over 3 tablespoons light muscovado sugar and cook until dissolved and the bananas are browning around the edges. Add the grated rind and juice of 1 lime, cook for 1 minute, then serve with the ice cream.

white choc & raspberry castles

Serves **6**
Preparation time **30 minutes**,
  plus freezing

750 ml (1¼ pints) **strawberry
  ice cream**
250 g (8 oz) **white chocolate**,
  broken into pieces
400 g (13 oz) **raspberries**

Line 6 small straight-sided individual china dishes or metal pudding moulds with clingfilm, then press a thick layer of ice cream into the base of each, then top with two small scoops. Freeze for 2–3 hours until firm.

Melt the chocolate (see page 11). Cut 6 strips of paper the circumference of the dish and 2.5 cm (1 inch) higher than the top of the dish. Spread the chocolate over the paper strips so that it covers the base and two short ends with a wavy, jagged edge to the second long side, just in from the paper edge.

Lift the ice cream quickly out of the moulds using the clingfilm, then peel off the clingfilm. Wrap one of the chocolate-covered strips around the side of the refrozen ice cream so that the chocolate touches the ice cream and the paper is on the outside. Repeat with the other moulded ice creams. Return to the freezer for 2 hours.

Reserve a few raspberries to decorate each castle. Purée the remainder of the raspberries and sieve, if liked. Drizzle the purée over 6 serving plates. Remove the ice creams from the freezer and peel away the paper. Transfer a castle to the centre of each serving plate and decorate with a few raspberries.

For brandy snap baskets with summer berries, use 500 g (1 lb) frozen mixed summer berry fruits instead of the raspberries. Reserve half the fruit and purée the rest, drizzling over 6 serving plates. Instead of making the castles, put the remaining fruit in 6 bought brandy-snap baskets and arrange on the plates with a scoop each of vanilla ice cream. Decorate with mint leaves.

key lime pie

Serves **8**
Preparation time **30 minutes**,
  plus chilling
Cooking time **15–20 minutes**

200 g (7 oz) **digestive
  biscuits**, crushed
4 tablespoons **caster sugar**
6 tablespoons **unsalted
  butter**, melted
3 **eggs**, separated
400 g (13 oz) can **full-fat
  condensed milk**
125 ml (4 fl oz) freshly
  squeezed **lime juice**
1 tablespoon **lemon juice**
2 teaspoons grated **lime rind**

Topping
250 ml (8 fl oz) **double cream**
1 tablespoon **icing sugar**
vanilla extract
lime slices, to decorate
  (optional)

Mix together the biscuit crumbs, half the sugar and the melted butter and press over the bottom and up the sides of a greased 23 cm (9 inch) springform tin. Refrigerate while making the filling.

Beat the egg yolks lightly together until creamy. Add the condensed milk, lime and lemon juice and lime rind and beat until well mixed and slightly thickened. In another bowl, beat the egg whites until stiff. Add the remainder of the sugar and continue beating until the meringue holds soft peaks (see page 10). Use a large metal spoon to fold the meringue mixture gently but thoroughly into the lime mixture.

Spoon the filling into the crumb crust and smooth the top. Bake in a preheated oven, 160°C (325°F), Gas Mark 3, for 15–20 minutes or until the filling is just firm and lightly browned on top. When cool, refrigerate the pie for at least 3 hours, until it is well chilled.

Whip the cream until it begins to thicken. Add the icing sugar and vanilla extract and continue whipping until it forms thick swirls. Spread the cream over the top of the chilled pie. Decorate with twisted lime slices, if liked. Remove the side of the pan just before serving and serve well chilled.

For no-bake key lime pie, make the biscuit crumb case as above. Whip 300 ml (½ pint) double cream until it forms soft swirls. Fold in 400 g (13 oz) condensed milk, then whisk in the grated rind and juice of 3 limes until thick. Pour into the biscuit case, spread into an even layer, then chill for at least 4 hours. Serve sliced, sprinkled with lime rind curls.

last-minute quickies

chocolate apple pancakes

Serves **4**

Preparation time **10 minutes**

Cooking time **7–8 minutes**

40 g (1½ oz) **unsalted butter**

3 **dessert apples**, cored and thickly sliced

2 large pinches **ground cinnamon**

4 **ready-made pancakes**, about 20 cm (8 inches) in diameter

4 tablespoons **chocolate and hazelnut spread**

icing sugar, for dusting

Melt half the butter in a large frying pan, then add the apples and fry for 3–4 minutes, stirring and turning until hot and lightly browned. Sprinkle with cinnamon.

Separate the pancakes, then spread with chocolate spread. Divide the apples among the pancakes, spooning them on to cover half of each pancake. Fold the uncovered sides over the apples.

Heat the remaining butter in the frying pan, add the pancakes and fry for a couple of minutes on each side to warm the pancakes through. Transfer to shallow plates and dust with sifted icing sugar.

For peach melba pancakes, fry 2 large, thickly sliced peaches in the butter instead of the apples, omitting the cinnamon. Spread the pancakes with 4 tablespoons raspberry jam, then add the peaches and fold. Warm through, then serve sprinkled with fresh raspberries, a dusting of icing sugar and a scoop of ice cream.

poached peaches & raspberries

Serves **6**
Preparation time **15 minutes**
Cooking time **25 minutes**

250 ml (8 fl oz) **water**
150 ml (¼ pint) **marsala** or
  sweet sherry
75 g (3 oz) **caster sugar**
1 **vanilla pod**
6 **peaches**, halved and pitted
150 g (5 oz) **fresh
  raspberries**

Pour the measured water and marsala or sherry into a saucepan, then add the sugar. Slit the vanilla pod lengthways and scrape out the black seeds from inside the pod. Add these to the water with the pod, then gently heat the mixture until the sugar has dissolved.

Place the peach halves in an overproof dish so that they sit together snugly. Pour over the hot syrup, then cover and cook in a preheated oven, 180°F (350°F), Gas Mark 4, for 20 minutes.

Scatter over the raspberries. Serve the fruit either warm or cold. Spoon into serving bowls and decorate with the vanilla pod cut into thin strips.

For poached prunes with vanilla, make the sugar syrup as above, then add 250 g (8 oz) dried pitted prunes instead of the peaches. Cover and simmer as above, then serve warm with spoonfuls of crème fraîche and 4 crumbled amaretti biscuits.

tamarind & mango sundae

Serves **4**
Preparation time **10 minutes**,
  plus cooling
Cooking time **8 minutes**

25 g (1 oz) **tamarind paste**
75 g (3 oz) **light muscovado
  sugar**
2 tablespoons **golden syrup**
grated rind and juice of 1 **lime**,
  plus extra pared **lime rind**,
  to decorate (optional)
150 ml (¼ pint) **water**
2 teaspoons **cornflour**
15 g (½ oz) **unsalted butter**
1 large **mango**, pitted, peeled
  and cut into strips
12 scoops **vanilla ice cream**

Put the tamarind paste, sugar and golden syrup in a small saucepan. Add the lime rind and juice and the measured water and bring to the boil, stirring until the sugar has dissolved. Simmer for 5 minutes.

Mix the cornflour with a little extra water in a cup, then add to the sauce with the butter, bring back to the boil and heat, stirring until thickened. Set aside to cool for 10 minutes.

Divide the mango and ice cream among 4 glass dishes, then drizzle a little of the sauce over the top and decorate with extra lime rind curls, if liked. Serve the remaining sauce in a small jug.

For tamarind & banana yogurts, make the tamarind sauce as above and leave until completely cold. Roughly chop 3 bananas and mix with 400 g (13 oz) Greek yogurt. Add the cooled tamarind sauce and mix briefly for a marbled effect. Spoon into glass dishes and serve.

pain perdu with mixed berries

Serves **4**
Preparation time **10 minutes**
Cooking time **10 minutes**

4 thick slices **brioche**
2 **eggs**
6 tablespoons **milk**
50 g (2 oz) **unsalted butter**
150 g (5 oz) **Greek yogurt**
250 g (8 oz) **raspberries**
100 g (3½ oz) **blueberries**
icing sugar, for dusting, or
    maple syrup

Cut each slice of brioche into two triangles. Beat the eggs and milk in a shallow bowl with a fork.

Heat half the butter in a frying pan. Quickly dip the bread, a triangle at a time, into the egg mixture, then put as many as you can get into the frying pan. Cook over a moderate heat until the underside is golden. Turn over and cook the second side, then lift out of the pan and keep hot.

Heat the remaining butter in the pan and dip and cook the remaining brioche triangles.

Arrange 2 triangles per serving on plates, top with spoonfuls of yogurt, a scattering of berries and a light dusting of sifted icing sugar or a drizzle of maple syrup. Serve immediately.

For spiced pain perdu with apricots, simmer 150 g (5 oz) ready-to-eat dried apricots with the juice of 1 orange and 125 ml (4 fl oz) water for 10 minutes until tender. Cut 4 slices of fruit bread in half. Mix the egg and milk as above with ¼ teaspoon ground cinnamon, then dip and fry the fruit bread as above. Arrange on plates with 150 g (5 oz) Greek yogurt and warm apricot compôte.

green fruit salad

300 g (10 oz) **seedless green grapes**, halved

4 **kiwifruits**, peeled, quartered and sliced

2 ripe **pears,** peeled, cored and sliced

4 **passion fruits**, halved

4 tablespoons **concentrated elderflower cordial**

4 tablespoons **water**

300 g (10 oz) **Greek yogurt**

2 tablespoons **runny honey**

Put the grapes, kiwifruits and pears in a bowl. Using a teaspoon, scoop the seeds from 3 of the passion fruits into the bowl. Mix 2 tablespoons of the cordial with the measured water and drizzle over the salad. Gently toss together and spoon into 6 glass tumblers.

Stir the remaining undiluted cordial into the yogurt, then mix in the honey. Spoon into the glasses. Decorate with the remaining passion fruit seeds and serve.

For ruby fruit salad, mix 300 g (10 oz) halved seedless red grapes with 150 g (5 oz) fresh raspberries and 150 g (5 oz) sliced strawberries. Sprinkle with the seeds from ½ pomegranate, then drizzle with 6 tablespoons red grape juice. Mix the yogurt with honey only, then spoon over the fruit salad. Decorate with a few extra pomegranate seeds.

sweet soufflé omelette

Serves **4**
Preparation time **15 minutes**
Cooking time **10 minutes**

375 g (12 oz) **strawberries**,
   hulled and thickly sliced, plus
   extra to decorate
2 tablespoons **redcurrant jelly**
2 teaspoons **balsamic
   vinegar**
5 **eggs**, separated
4 tablespoons **icing sugar**,
   sifted
25 g (1 oz) **unsalted butter**

Warm the strawberries, redcurrant jelly and vinegar together in a saucepan until the jelly has just melted.

Meanwhile, whisk the egg whites into stiff, moist-looking peaks. Mix the egg yolks with 1 tablespoon of the sugar, then fold into the egg whites.

Heat the butter in a large frying pan, add the egg mixture and cook over a medium heat for 3–4 minutes until the underside is golden. Quickly transfer the pan to a hot grill and cook for 2–3 minutes until the top is browned and the centre still slightly soft, making sure that the pan handle is away from the heat.

Spoon the warm strawberry mixture over the omelette, fold in half and dust with the remaining sugar. Cut into 4 and serve immediately with extra strawberries.

For sweet soufflé omelette with peaches & blueberries, put 2 ripe peaches, sliced, into a saucepan together with 100 g (3½ oz) blueberries, 2 tablespoons redcurrant jelly and 2 tablespoons lemon juice. Warm together, then make the sweet soufflé omelette as above, spoon over the warm fruit and serve immediately.

white choc & raspberry tiramisu

Serves **6**
Preparation time **20 minutes**

3 level teaspoons **instant coffee**
7 tablespoons **icing sugar**
250 ml (8 fl oz) **boiling water**
12 **sponge finger biscuits**, about 100 g (3½ oz)
250 g (8 oz) **mascarpone cheese**
150 ml (¼ pint) **double cream**
3 tablespoons **kirsch** (optional)
250 g (8 oz) **fresh raspberries**
75 g (3 oz) **white chocolate**, diced

Put the coffee and 4 tablespoons of the icing sugar into a shallow dish, then pour on the measured boiling water and mix until dissolved. Dip 6 biscuits, one at a time, into the coffee mixture, then crumble into the bases of 6 glass tumblers.

Put the mascarpone into a bowl with the remaining icing sugar, then gradually whisk in the cream until smooth. Stir in the kirsch, if using, then divide half the mixture between the glasses.

Crumble half the raspberries over the top of the mascarpone in the glasses, then sprinkle with half the chocolate. Dip the remaining biscuits in the coffee mix, crumble and add to the glasses. Then add the rest of the mascarpone and the remaining raspberries, this time left whole, finishing with a sprinkling of the chocolate. Serve immediately or chill until required.

For classic tiramisu, omit the raspberries and white chocolate from the layers. Mix the mascarpone with the cream and 3 tablespoons Kahlua coffee liqueur or brandy, then layer in one large glass dish with the coffee-dipped sponge finger biscuits and 75 g (3 oz) diced plain dark chocolate.

banana & muscovado ripples

Serves **4**
Preparation time **5 minutes**,
  plus standing

2 ripe **bananas**
juice of ½ **lemon**
15 g (½ oz) **crystallized** or
  glacé ginger, finely chopped,
  plus extra to decorate
150 g (5 oz) **low-fat natural**
  yogurt
8 teaspoons dark **muscovado**
  sugar

Toss the bananas in a little lemon juice and mash on a plate with a fork. Add the ginger and yogurt and mix together. Spoon one-third of the mixture into the bases of 4 small dessert glasses.

Sprinkle 1 teaspoon of the sugar over each dessert. Spoon half of the remaining banana mixture on top, then repeat with a second layer of sugar. Complete the layers with the remaining banana mixture and decorate with a little extra ginger, cut into slightly larger pieces.

Leave the puddings to stand for 10–15 minutes for the sugar to dissolve and form a syrupy layer between the layers of banana yogurt. Serve with dainty biscuits, if liked.

For banana, apricot & cardamom ripples, cook 100 g (3½ oz) ready-to-eat dried apricots with 150 ml (¼ pint) water and 2 roughly crushed cardamom pods, adding the pods and their black seeds, in a covered saucepan for 10 minutes until tender. Remove and discard the cardamom pods, then purée the mixture with 3 tablespoons fresh orange juice. Cool, then layer with banana and the yogurt mix as above. This can be served immediately.

summer fruit gratin

Serves **4**
Preparation time **10 minutes**
Cooking time **20 minutes**

2 ripe **peaches**, pitted
and sliced
4 ripe **red plums**, pitted
and sliced
150 g (5 oz) mixed
raspberries and
blackberries (or all
raspberries)
200 g (7 oz) **mascarpone
cheese**
4 tablespoons **caster sugar**
2 tablespoons **double cream**
grated rind of **1 lime**

Arrange all the fruit in a shallow ovenproof dish. Mix the mascarpone with 2 tablespoons of the sugar, the cream and the lime rind, then spoon over the fruit and spread into an even layer.

Sprinkle the top with the remaining sugar, then put on a baking sheet and cook in a preheated oven, 190°C (375°F), Gas Mark 5, for 15 minutes until the cheese has softened and the sugar topping has caramelized. Serve immediately.

For tropical fruit gratin, arrange slices of 1 large mango in the dish with 1 sliced papaya and 150 g (5 oz) blueberries. Top with the mascarpone mix and bake as above.

baked apples & flapjack crumble

Serves **4**
Preparation time **15 minutes**
Cooking time **20–25 minutes**

4 **dessert apples**, halved and
  cored
75 g (3 oz) **raisins**
4 tablespoons **golden syrup**
6 tablespoons **apple juice**
  or **water**
50 g (2 oz) **plain flour**
50 g (2 oz) **rolled oats**
50 g (2 oz) **light muscovado
  sugar**
50 g (2 oz) **unsalted butter**,
  at room temperature, diced
2 tablespoons **sunflower
  seeds**
2 tablespoons **sesame seeds**

Arrange the apples, cut side up, in a shallow ovenproof
dish. Divide the raisins among the apples, pressing
them into the core cavity. Drizzle with 2 tablespoons
of the golden syrup and add the apple juice or water
to the base of the dish.

Put the flour, oats, sugar and butter into a small bowl
and rub in the butter with fingertips until the mixture
resembles fine breadcrumbs. Stir in the seeds. Spoon
the crumble over the top of the apples and mound up.
Drizzle with the remaining syrup.

Cook in a preheated oven, 180°C (350°F), Gas Mark
4, for 20–25 minutes until the crumble is golden and
the apples are soft. Serve warm with scoops of vanilla
ice cream or crème fraîche.

For plum & muesli crumble, halve 10 plums and
place them, cut side up, in an ovenproof dish. Drizzle
with 2 tablespoons honey and add 6 tablespoons red
grape juice or water to the base of the dish. Make the
crumble, using 75 g (3 oz) of muesli instead of the
oats and seeds. Bake and serve as above.

hot caribbean fruit salad

Serves **4**
Preparation time **15 minutes**
Cooking time **6–7 minutes**

50 g (2 oz) **unsalted butter**
50 g (2 oz) **light muscovado sugar**
1 large **papaya**, halved, deseeded, peeled and sliced
1 large **mango**, pitted, peeled and sliced
½ **pineapple**, cored, peeled and cut into chunks
400 ml (14 fl oz) can **full-fat coconut milk**
grated rind and juice of 1 **lime**

Heat the butter in a large frying pan, add the sugar and heat gently until just dissolved. Add all the fruit and cook for 2 minutes, then pour in the coconut milk, half the lime rind and all the juice.

Heat gently for 4–5 minutes, then serve warm in shallow bowls, sprinkled with the remaining lime rind.

For flamed Caribbean fruit salad, omit the coconut milk and add 3 tablespoons dark or white rum. When the rum is bubbling, flame with a long match and stand well back. When the flames have subsided, add the lime rind and juice and serve with scoops of vanilla ice cream.

mini baked alaskas

Serves **4**
Preparation time **15 minutes**,
   plus freezing time
Cooking time **5 minutes**

4 slices **jam Swiss roll** or
   4 trifle sponges, separated,
   with the corners trimmed off
4 scoops **strawberry and
   vanilla ice cream** or **vanilla
   ice cream**
2 **egg whites**
50 g (2 oz) **caster sugar**
175 g (6 oz) **frozen summer
   fruits**, just defrosted or
   warmed in a small saucepan

Arrange the slices of Swiss roll or trifle sponge, well spaced apart, on a baking sheet, then top each with a scoop of ice cream. Put into the freezer for 10 minutes (or longer if you have time).

Whisk the egg whites in a large bowl until stiff, moist-looking peaks form. Gradually whisk in the sugar, a teaspoon at a time, and continue whisking for a few minutes until thick and glossy (see page 10).

Take the sponge and ice cream from the freezer and quickly swirl the meringue over the top and sides to cover completely. Cook in a preheated oven, 200°C (400°F), Gas Mark 6, for 5 minutes until the peaks are golden brown, the meringue is cooked through and the ice cream only just beginning to soften.

Transfer the baked Alaskas to shallow serving bowls and spoon the summer fruit around the base of the desserts. Serve immediately.

For cappuccino Alaskas, use chocolate Swiss roll (choose one without a chocolate outside coating) instead of the jam Swiss roll or trifle sponges. Top each slice with a scoop of coffee ice cream, then the meringue as above. When baked, dust lightly with sifted drinking chocolate powder and serve immediately.

caramelized clementines with bay

Serves **4**
Preparation time **10 minutes**
Cooking time **12 minutes**

250 g (8 oz) **granulated sugar**
250 ml (8 fl oz) **cold water**
8 **clementines**
4 small **fresh bay leaves**
6 tablespoons **boiling water**

Put the sugar and measured cold water in a saucepan and heat gently, stirring very occasionally until the sugar has completely dissolved.

Meanwhile, peel the clementines and, leaving them whole, place in a heavy glass serving bowl or mixing bowl with the bay leaves.

Increase the heat once the sugar has dissolved and boil the syrup for 8–10 minutes, without stirring and keeping a close watch on it until it begins to change colour, first becoming pale golden around the edges, then a rich golden colour all over.

Take the pan off the heat, then add the measured boiling water, a tablespoon at a time, standing well back in case the syrup spits. Tilt the pan to mix but don't stir. Once the bubbles have subsided, pour the hot syrup over the clementines and bay leaves. Leave to cool, then serve the dessert with scoops of crème fraîche or cream.

For caramelized clementines with whole spices, omit the bay leaves and add 2 whole star anise or the equivalent in pieces, 1 cinnamon stick, halved, and 3 cloves to the clementines. Make the syrup as above, then pour it over the spices and fruit.

mulled wine pears

Serves **6**
Preparation time **10 minutes**
Cooking time **12 minutes**

300 ml (½ pint) cheap **red wine**
200 ml (7 fl oz) **water**
rind and juice of 1 **orange**
1 **cinnamon stick**, broken into large pieces
6 **cloves**
2 small **fresh bay leaves**
75 g (3 oz) **caster sugar**
6 **pears**
3 teaspoons **cornflour**

Pour the wine and measured water into a saucepan that will hold the pears snugly. Cut the orange rind into thin strips, then add to the pan with the orange juice, spices, bay leaves and sugar. Heat gently until the sugar has dissolved.

Peel the pears, leaving the stalks on, then add them to the red wine syrup. Simmer gently for 10 minutes, turning the pears several times so that they cook and colour evenly.

Lift the pears out of the pan and put on a plate. Mix the cornflour with a little water in a cup, then stir into the wine syrup and bring to the boil, stirring until thickened and smooth. Add the pears and leave to cool.

Transfer to shallow dishes with a rim and serve with spoonfuls of crème fraîche or cream.

For apples with cider punch, use sweet cider in place of the red wine, then add the orange rind and juice, spices and sugar as above, omitting the bay leaves. Dissolve the sugar, then add 6 dessert apples, peeled, cored and quartered. Simmer for 5 minutes until just tender, then thicken the syrup with cornflour as above.

moroccan baked figs with yogurt

Serves **4**
Preparation time **10 minutes**
Cooking time **10 minutes**

8 **fresh figs**, rinsed in cold
water
About 3 teaspoons **rose
water**
4 tablespoons **runny honey**
50 g (2 oz) **unsalted butter**
250 g (8 oz) **Greek yogurt**
a little **Turkish delight**, roughly
chopped

Cut a cross in the top of each fig and open out the cut
to halfway through the fruit. Arrange the figs in a small
roasting tin or shallow ovenproof dish. Add a few drops
of rose water to each fig, then drizzle with 3 tablespoons
of the honey and dot with the butter.

Bake in a preheated oven, 190°C (375°F), Gas Mark
5, for 8–10 minutes until the figs are hot but still firm.
Meanwhile, mix the yogurt with the remaining honey
and gradually mix in a little of the remaining rose water
to taste.

Transfer the figs to shallow serving dishes and serve
with spoonfuls of yogurt sprinkled with Turkish delight.

For orange & pistachio baked apricots, arrange
12 fresh apricots, halved, in a roasting tin. Add a few
drops of orange flower water to each apricot half, then
drizzle with 3 tablespoons honey and sprinkle with
40 g (1½ oz) halved pistachio nuts. Dot with 50 g
(2 oz) butter and bake as above. Serve with 250 g
(8 oz) Greek yogurt flavoured with 1 tablespoon
honey and orange flower water to taste.

white chocolate fondue with fruit

Serves **4**
Preparation time **10 minutes**
Cooking time **5 minutes**

200 g (7 oz) good-quality
white chocolate, broken into
pieces
300 ml (½ pint) **double cream**
2 tablespoons **kirsch**
2 **peaches**, cut into chunks
250 g (8 oz) large
raspberries
375 g (12 oz) **strawberries**,
halved
small bunch of **seedless red
grapes**

Melt the chocolate together with the cream in a bowl set over a pan of gently simmering water (see page 11). Stir in the kirsch.

Arrange all the fruit on individual serving plates with forks or skewers for spearing the pieces.

Keep the fondue warm over a fondue burner while you dip and eat, or spoon the fondue into individual bowls, if preferred.

For dark chocolate & vanilla fondue, heat 200 g (7 oz) plain dark chocolate, 300 ml (½ pint) double cream, 4 tablespoons light muscovado sugar and 1 teaspoon vanilla essence together, stirring until smooth. Serve with 2 peaches, cut into chunks, 2 red-skinned dessert apples, cut into chunks, and 125 g (4 oz) marshmallows.

grilled strawberry zabaglione

Serves **4**
Preparation time **10 minutes**
Cooking time **10 minutes**

500 g (1 lb) **strawberries**,
  halved or quartered,
  depending on size
3 **egg yolks**
50 g (2 oz) **caster sugar**
6 tablespoons **dry** or **sweet
  sherry**
4 teaspoons **icing sugar**

Divide the strawberries among 4 shallow 300 ml (½ pint) ovenproof dishes, or use a large 1.2 litre (2 pint) dish if preferred.

Put the egg yolks, sugar and 4 tablespoons of the sherry in a large bowl and set over a pan of simmering water. Cook the mixture, whisking continuously using a hand-held electric whisk (or rotary hand or balloon whisk), for 5 minutes until the mixture is very thick and frothy and almost half-fills the bowl.

Add the remaining sherry and cook for a few more minutes until thick once more. Pour the mixture over the strawberries and sift the icing sugar over the top.

Cook under a preheated hot grill for 3–4 minutes until golden or caramelize the sugar with a cook's blowtorch. Serve immediately.

For fruit salad zabaglione, divide 125 g (4 oz) fresh raspberries, 125 g (4 oz) halved seedless red or green grapes and 2 peeled and diced kiwifruits among 4 glass tumblers. Make the zabaglione with 6 tablespoons dry white wine instead of sherry, and when just cooked pour over the fruit but don't grill.

caramelized blueberries & custard

Serves **6**
Preparation time **10 minutes**
Cooking time **5 minutes**

150 g (5 oz) **granulated sugar**
3 tablespoons **cold water**
2 tablespoons **boiling water**
150 g (5 oz) **fresh** (not frozen) **blueberries**
400 g (13 oz) **fromage frais**
425 g (14 oz) can or carton **custard**

Put the sugar and measured cold water into a frying pan and heat gently, stirring very occasionally until the sugar has completely dissolved. Bring to the boil and cook for 3–4 minutes, without stirring, until the syrup is just changing colour and is golden around the edges.

Add the measured boiling water, standing well back as the syrup will spit, then tilt the pan to mix. Add the blueberries and cook for 1 minute. Take the pan off the heat and set aside to cool slightly (maybe while you eat your main course).

Mix the fromage frais and custard together, spoon into small dishes, then spoon the blueberry mixture over the top. Serve immediately, with baby meringues if liked.

For banana custards, make the caramel as above, then add 2 sliced bananas instead of the blueberries. Cool slightly, then spoon over the custard and fromage frais mixture. Decorate with a little grated plain dark chocolate.

citrus refresher

Serves **4**
Preparation time **10 minutes**
Cooking time **6–7 minutes**

150 ml (¼ pint) chilled **orange
  juice** from a carton
150 ml (¼ pint) **water**
125 g (4 oz) **caster sugar**
juice of ½ **lemon**
2 **ruby grapefruit**
4 **oranges** (a mix of **ordinary**
  and **blood oranges**, if
  available)
1 **orange-fleshed melon**
½ **pomegranate**

Pour the orange juice and measured water into a
saucepan, add the sugar and heat gently until the
sugar has dissolved, then simmer for 5 minutes until
syrupy. Take off the heat and mix in the lemon juice.

Cut a slice off the top and bottom of each grapefruit,
then cut away the rest of the peel in downward slices
using a small serrated knife. Holding the fruit over
a bowl, cut between the membranes to release the
segments. Cut a slice off the top and bottom of the
oranges, then cut away the rest of the peel. Cut into
segments and add to the bowl.

Cut the melon in half, scoop out the seeds, then cut
away the peel and dice the flesh. Add to the citrus fruit,
then pour over the syrup. Flex the pomegranate to
release the seeds, sprinkle over the salad, then chill
until ready to serve.

For orange & fig refresher, make the syrup as above.
Omit the grapefruit and increase the number of
oranges to 6. Cut 4 fresh figs into wedges, peel and
add to the oranges. Add the sugar syrup and sprinkle
with some fresh mint leaves. Serve chilled.

barbecued bananas

Serves **4**
Preparation time **5 minutes**
Cooking time **10 minutes**

4 bananas
4 tablespoons **rum** (or
   Amaretto liqueur, brandy
   or **sherry**)
grated rind of **1 lime**

To serve
4 scoops **vanilla ice cream**
8 **ratafia biscuits**, crumbled

Cook the bananas still in their skins on the barbecue for 8–10 minutes as the heat from the embers begins to lose its fierceness, until the skins have blackened and the flesh is softened. Alternatively, bake for the same period in a preheated oven, 200°C (400°F), Gas Mark 6.

Split the skins lengthways and place a banana in its skin on each of 4 serving plates. Drizzle the rum inside the baked banana and sprinkle with the lime rind. Serve at once, with scoops of ice cream and the crumbled ratafia biscuits.

For Jamaican banana parcels, peel 4 bananas, halve lengthways and divide between 4 pieces of foil. Dot with 40 g (1½ oz) unsalted butter, 2 tablespoons light muscovado sugar, the juice of 1 lime and 2 tablespoons rum. Seal the foil well so that none of the ingredients can escape, then add to the barbecue and cook for 5–8 minutes until the bananas are softened. Serve warm with ice cream.

index

acknowledgements

Executive Editor: Nicola Hill
Senior Editor: Fiona Robertson
Executive Art Editor: Leigh Jones
Designer: Jo Tapper
Photographer: Will Heap
Home Economist: Sara Lewis
Props Stylist: Liz Hippisley
Production Controller: Carolin Stransky

Special Photography: © Octopus Publishing Group Limited/Will Heap
Other Photography: © Octopus Publishing Group Limited/Gareth Sambridge 20, 22, 29, 35, 49, 73, 125, 151, 179; /Ian Wallace 81, 85, 89, 93, 97, 101, 107, 121, 126, 127, 131, 183, 193; /Jeremy Hopley 143, 147; /Lis Parsons 77, 135, 139, 154, 208; /Stephen Conroy 111, 169, 173, 177, 188; /William Lingwood 105.